soul friends

What Every Woman Needs
to Grow in Her Faith

dr. leslie parrott

ZONDERVAN®

ZONDERVAN

Soul Friends
Copyright © 2014 The Foundation for Healthy Relationships

This title is also available as a Zondervan ebook. Visit www.zondervan.com/ebooks.

Requests for information should be addressed to:
Zondervan, 3900 *Sparks Dr. SE, Grand Rapids, Michigan* 49546

ISBN 978-0-310-27330-1

Published in association with Yates & Yates, LLP, Attorneys and Counselors, Orange, California, and Result Source, Inc., San Diego, California.

Cover photo: *Dan Davis Photography*
Interior design: *Katherine Lloyd, The DESK*

First Printing February 2015 / Printed in the United States of America

For Sara Grace
Your mom is a Soul Friend,
and you are a Daughter of the Heart.

contents

part three
crisis

part four
communion

acknowledgments

Sincere thanks to ...

Lori Vanden Bosch and Sandy Vander Zicht, my brilliant editorial team, whose grace and grit infused this process with joy. I count you each as soul friends.

Tom Dean and the rest of the Zondervan marketing team, for capturing the spirit of this book.

Our dear Seattle friends Kristin and Brandon Hill, for your heartfelt and incredibly creative investment in this project.

Joyce Ondersma and Jackie Aldridge, for all the TLC along the way (and for the fragrant bouquet that arrived at just the right time).

Sealy Yates, for ever-and-always being my champion as I seek to be faithful to my calling through words.

Ryan Farmer and Kevin Small, true partners in our commitment and calling. I couldn't be more honored by your investment of time and talents (or more impressed by your savvy).

My husband, Les, whose wit, wisdom, and loyal love is the very landscape of my life. And to our sons, John and Jackson, whom we adore together. Thank you for sharing every minute of this process and for accommodating those monastic Appassionato moments that created space for me to write.

Mom and Aunt Jill, whose unwavering care form the bedrock of my life and whose prayers have graced every page of this book.

My Friday Friends, who have wholeheartedly served as my sisterhood of saints for a dozen years: Arlys, Bonnie, Joy, Lori, Sandy, and Tami. There aren't words to say thank you enough.

And more than ever, to the soul friends whose stories fill these pages and whose love and faith have shown me the way forward on my own Jesus journey, I thank you from the bottom of my heart.

invitation

I want you to get out there and walk — better yet,
run! — on the road God called you to travel.

Ephesians 4:1

I'm not a map person. I have never been skilled with a compass. When I navigate, I tend to use landmarks and intuition, feeling my way toward my destination. The author Herman Melville once said, "It is not down on any map; true places never are." To that my heart says, *amen*. But after wading through the theological maps of the spiritual journey, after mulling over the distilled wisdom of great spiritual thinkers and mapmakers such as theologian Søren Kierkegaard, I began to see the spiritual journey in terms of four major landmarks: Quest, Calling, Crisis, and Communion.

At the beginning we are on a Quest. Each one of us is caught up in following our heart further and deeper down the pathway of our own feelings, dreams, and desires. This stage of life is lived on the surface; we are preoccupied with finding the key to our own happily-ever-after, whether it is in the eyes of someone who loves us, little ones who depend on us, or a job that defines us. We are consumed with understanding and pursuing the "desires of our heart." Inevitably some of our dreams are fulfilled and some of them die. Either way, we experience the ache of loss, when the dream fulfilled doesn't satisfy or the dream denied leaves a howling gap.

The next movement is into a more profound place of faith. I think of it as the *Calling.* When we fail to find the key to the "desires of our heart" (or even more quickly, when we do find it, and yet our heart still throbs with desire), we travel forward. At this point, as followers of Jesus, we begin to willingly lay aside our own desires and take a "leap of faith" further into a passionate relationship with Christ. Now our heart's truest desire becomes obedience to the will and purposes of God. At this stage we pour ourselves into the work God has called us to with all the energy, will, and discernment we have. It's that moment when Jesus says to Peter, after a disappointing night of fishing with no catch, and a morning miracle of fish so bountiful they threaten to burst the nets and sink the boat, "Come with me. I'll make a new kind of fisherman out of you" (Matthew 4:19). And we drop the nets that were poised to catch our dreams, whether empty or full, and follow Jesus willingly, into the unknown, knowing only that he is our Way.

Ultimately we find ourselves once again on the move into a new and deeper inward experience; it's a place I call *Crisis.* After coming face-to-face with suffering or our own limitations as we seek to live out this life of obedience to God's call, we cry out with the apostle Paul: "What I don't understand about myself is that I decide one way, but then I act another ... The moment I decide to do good, sin is there to trip me up. I truly delight in God's commands, but it's pretty obvious not all of me joins in that delight. Parts of me covertly rebel, and just when I least expect it, they take charge" (Romans 7:15, 21–23).

We begin to accurately understand our own inner condition, and we come to realize that the ultimate surrender is not as simple as just deciding to live in obedience to God's law, but instead is turning our very selves over to be completely transformed by God. Only when this miracle occurs can we become completely surrendered to the revealed purposes of God. Surrender like this takes us to the center of an intimacy with God so deep that it has truly become *Communion.* At this level, our life is so defined by knowing God and being known by God, that our inner complexities have been overshadowed by God's grace. Surrender to the will of God is now our strength rather than our struggle. And with Paul we can say, "I delight in weaknesses ... For when I am weak, then I am strong" (2 Corinthians 12:10 NIV).

Of course, these stages overlap and intersect. And we might think we are "done" with a stage only to be thrown back into it. So while this book is divided into four neat sections, the stories and experiences aren't so easily divisible. The Quest often contains our Calling, and through our Quest and our Calling and our times of Crisis we find moments of Communion with God. Like the wheel of life, the stages turn and spin and push us forward. But through it all there remains a God-given constant: the body of Christ, or to use the ancient Apostles' Creed words, "the community of saints." And for me this especially includes my soul friends, the sisters in the faith traveling alongside me.

An ancient Gaelic phrase, *anam chara*, literally means "soul friend." Long ago in the Celtic world, every village appointed a woman to serve as midwife in birth and mourner in death. This beloved *anam chara* worked tenderly in her village to nurture and care for people undergoing life's major transitions. Hers was a sacred role. Today we all step reverently into that role when we enter into the sacred task of tending to one another's lives through deep-spirited friendship. We stand beside one another in moments of inward mourning and in the miracles of spiritual birth as we undergo the formation of our faith.

Somewhere along life's journey I have come to understand that, as a woman, friendships are essential to the formation of my faith. Especially in the midst of those moments when the tears are flowing involuntarily—as if somehow the dry soil of my soul has triggered some cosmic sprinkler system designed by my Master Gardener.

The truth is, as women, we are uniquely designed by God to lean into soul friendships. This isn't just a spiritual and emotional difference but one that is woven into the very chemistry of our bodies. In fact, as babes in the womb, before we reach the end of the first trimester of development, boys and girls experience a radical divergence in brain development. Although we start out essentially identical, at the end of the eighth week, male brains are bathed in testosterone, which damages cells in the corpus callosum, a bundle of nerves connecting the left and right hemispheres of the brain. This brain change shows up in the capacity to connect communication and emotion. In girls, this nerve bundle is strongly developed, and so are the abilities of girls to be expressive of emotions and articulate in communication.

This design deep within us doesn't stop with our formation in the womb, but rather becomes more defined as we mature and develop through a trio of hormones that surge within us far more than they do in men: estrogen, progesterone, and prolactin. Like a three-stranded cord, these hormones create the need for deep connection, the capacity for feeling and empathy (even producing tear glands), and the desire to nurture and foster relationships around us (sometimes called "nesting"). Sociologist Carol Gilligan calls it our "web of connectedness."[1] And as women, we are so oriented toward attachment that we fear a rupture in relationship more than a loss of independence. In short, we have a God-given need for soul friendships that is more ancient than the Celtic world. And because of it, we can trust that there is great purpose and fulfillment in the give-and-take of these deep-spirited relationships.

Soul friends are found in predictable places — churches and small groups — and among predictable people — current friends and mentors. But they're sometimes people you wouldn't expect. I call them "hidden guides," individuals whose role in our lives may be hidden even to them, but who nevertheless have a deep impact on our growth and vitality.

A hidden guide might be a nurse in a hospital corridor whose wisdom in a time of need penetrates our hearts now and forever. It might be the author of a book (living or dead) whose

1. Carol Gilligan, *In a Different Voice: Psychological Theory and Women's Development* (Boston: Harvard University Press, 1982), 62.

words become signposts on our road. It might be someone who is on the periphery of our lives until we step into a situation—the birth of a preemie, a shocking diagnosis, a fresh vocational call—that connects us to their story.

Whether it's a hidden guide, a member of a small group, a friend we've had for years, or even a companion of the soul who reaches us through the pages of an ancient spiritual classic or a freshly written book, every soul friend holds the potential to embody grace, enabling us to take a next step in the unfolding journey of our lives.

I love learning the way Jesus loved teaching: through good stories. And that's why the spiritual classic *Hinds Feet on High Places* has deeply formed my own understanding of what it means to walk the journey of faith. Its author, Hannah Hurnard, a missionary who left her native England to serve in Israel for fifty years, writes a beautiful allegory centered on a lame and disfigured young woman named Much-Afraid. As Much-Afraid answers the call of her Good Shepherd to embark on a journey to the High Places, she takes the hands of her two companions, Suffering and Sorrow, for the arduous climb into the Kingdom of Love.

As the journey progresses, Much-Afraid builds many altars along the way, each time choosing to trust her Shepherd and obey him, even when it seems to require the surrender of her heart's desires. In the end, the little pebbles she has collected as memorials of these altars are transfigured into shining jewels that form her crown in the High Places of Love, and she herself is transformed into Grace and Glory. No longer lame, she has feet as nimble as a hind and can leap fearlessly about the cliff-edges of the High Places and back down into the Valley of Humiliation, where she can encourage others to start their own journey into the Kingdom of Love.

Much-Afraid (and of course the heart and hand behind her, Hannah Hurnard) has been a hidden guide on my own journey, one I turn to again and again, reading and rereading the story in seasons of great growth and of great sorrow. So meaningful was the story to me following my parents' divorce, and the compounding stress that resulted in physical disabilities for my mom, that I sent her a copy along with a little leather pouch filled with jewels. I wanted her to have tangible, symbolic reminders that her Good Shepherd was in the business of transforming each of her agonizing losses into something more beautiful than either of us could possibly imagine.

In fact, just as *Hinds Feet on High Places* has been *anam chara* to me and my mother (and may be to you as well), my hope is that you would receive *Soul Friends* in a similar way. I would be honored if we could take a small part of this formational journey together. Each of us falling in step for a time, becoming *anam chara*—agents of grace, transformation, and healing for one another as we move forward in faith; deeper into our experience of Quest, Calling, Crisis, and Communion; and further into the presence of the Holy Spirit in the relationships that surround us. Soul friend, will you join me in this incredible journey of faith and friendship?

Anne Lamott was in Seattle recently, giving a talk at my Aunt Jill's historic downtown church. During an engaging time of question and answer, she remarked offhandedly, "All we are really doing is just walking each other home." That single, powerful, compelling image is what guides me while I write these words: a sisterhood of traveling saints linked together, walking the Jesus journey, *anam chara*-walking each other home.

One last thought right here at the beginning. You may be thinking, "Well, it's easy enough for you to talk about soul friends. You obviously have a great (fill in the blank here: church, small group, friend, family, husband). But you can't begin to understand what it's like for me." And you're right; I can't. That is a true limitation of sharing this journey through the pages of a book. But what I do understand is this: all of us lead lives marked by relational imperfection, and some of us have endured genuine relational trauma.

Søren Kierkegaard, with all his brilliance regarding spiritual formation, was not immune. He had what he described as a "great earthquake" when he discovered that his own father, a believer who struggled with deep depression, had a history of sexual infidelity. I have had my own fair share of seasons of great upheaval, but perhaps they don't even come close to whatever it is that you have survived.

At the very least, all of us are surrounded by people, like us, whose flaws, quirks, and failures impact us in big and small ways on a daily basis. Friends and family love us and fail us simultaneously. I love what Paul says to the Corinthians, "And don't be wishing you were someplace else or with someone else. Where you are right now is God's place for you. Live and obey and love and believe right there" (1 Corinthians 7:17). The way my pastor, Richard Dahlstrom, preaches it is this: "*Context* is God's business." In other words, the surrounding circumstances or "setting" we find ourselves in is the milieu in which God will work his transformational art in us and through us, no matter how much it might seem otherwise. Our job is simply to trust and obey, and continue taking the risk to love and serve in whatever context God has placed us.

soul souvenirs

1. Can you relate to the landmarks of Quest, Calling, Crisis, and Communion when it comes to the faith journey? If so, in which place do you find yourself right now?

2. Can you think of a time when you either experienced the comfort of an *anam chara* or stepped into the role of *anam chara*, supporting a friend through a time of great joy or great sorrow? How was it a sacred experience for you?

part one

quest

Our desire to live questingly—to taste all that life has to offer of love, friendship, meaning, and adventure—runs deep. In so many ways it has less to do with our fantasy about what the world holds for us than it does with our dreams about what we bring to the world. We long to find buried treasure; but even more, we long to be a treasure for those who know and love us, our soul friends.

chapter 1

adventure
club

> *This resurrection life you received from God is not a timid, grave-tending life. It's adventurously expectant, greeting God with a childlike "What's next, Papa?"*   Romans 8:15

Ellie, the scrappy tomboy in Disney's movie *Up*, has the brave heart of an explorer. Inspired by tales of adventure, she dreams of journeying to Paradise Falls in South America. "It's like America, but South," she says with her adorable gap-toothed lisp. What I love most about Ellie is that no sooner has this dream-quest been birthed in her soul than she forms a "club." When Carl, the neighborhood boy (who is shy and timid but whose heart also shares the dream for great exploration), wanders into her "clubhouse," she immediately initiates him into the club, a ceremony completed by the pinning of a grape soda badge onto his chest. This initiation promptly costs him a broken arm (when he attempts to retrieve a lost balloon by walking across a precarious ceiling beam in a dilapidated old house), as if to underscore the true risk involved in an adventurous life.

Getting to Paradise Falls is Ellie's Quest. And yet, true to her gender, Ellie does not see this as an autonomous task, to be accomplished independently. She doesn't view this as her heroic moment to shine, but rather, she instinctively leans into the bonds of connection and relationship in the face of the challenge. Sociologists tell us that when it comes to any great challenge in life, women are eager to join the journey with each other, while men instinctively want everyone to see how they can go it alone. We have been uniquely hardwired by God to reach out before we forge ahead into our wild blue yonder. For us, as women, it really is "off *we* go!"

Well, as you probably already know, Ellie and Carl's little adventure club eventually led to the greatest adventure of their lives: a marriage. And in time, Ellie's Quest expanded to include the dream of having a baby. I love the scene of the young couple happily stretched out on a picnic blanket placed atop a grassy hillside. It is clearly a favorite spot they have visited on countless happy occasions. On this day they are studying the blue sky together, finding recognizable shapes in the cloud formations, when suddenly, for Ellie, all of the clouds shapes have rearranged themselves into babies. At first surprised, Carl soon joins in the joy of this new phase of Ellie's Quest.

But as the story unfolds, we discover that Ellie does not have the joy of giving birth to her own baby. And furthermore, she never makes it to Paradise Falls. Countless little setbacks and crises along life's road stymie the couple's quest ... until eventually illness and age steal Ellie away, even as they are on the verge of attaining the funds for their much-dreamed-of destination. What she did have along the way, however, was the adventure of loving and being loved. And here is the crux of it: Ellie's dream, although technically unfulfilled, expanded far beyond her, eventually transforming the lives of Carl and a neglected little "wilderness explorer," Russell. Ellie's life had moved beyond the fulfillment of her Quest, as ours must, and into the place of Calling, Crisis, and transforming, true Communion.

Whether our dreams (that form our own personal Quest) come true is not the point of this journey so much as the way God uses our lives to accomplish his purposes in ways that surpass our imagining. The truth is, it's the loving and being loved along the way which transforms us so completely that even the unfulfilled dreams become our pathway to joy rather than an occasion for sorrow. Our Quest, our Calling, and our Crisis always take place in the Communion of saints, chosen and gathered around us by our heavenly Father's hand.

Listen to these words of Bishop Bardsley from an old spiritual classic:

> When a soul sets out to find God it does not know whither it will come and by what path it will be led; but those who catch the vision are ready to follow the Lamb whithersoever He goeth, regardless of what that following may involve for them. And it is as they follow, obedient to what they have seen, in this spirit of joyful adventure that their path becomes clear before them, and they are given the power to fulfill their high calling. They are those who have the courage to break conventionalities, who care not at all what the world thinks of them because they

are entirely taken up with the tremendous realities of the soul and God.[2]

Oh, how I wish I could be there beside you right now holding a grape soda badge to safety-pin over your heart to mark this moment as an occasion of great consequence. Why? Because each one of us is invited into God's Adventure Club. And isn't grape soda the perfect symbol for true communion? Jesus tells us, "I am the Vine, you are the branches. When you're joined with me and I with you ... the harvest is sure to be abundant ... This is how my Father shows who he is — when you produce grapes, when you mature as my disciples" (John 15:5, 8).

Sisters, adventure is out there! Your Quest can become an instrument through which God works his transformational art within you and the seemingly random bystanders in the context around you, whoever they might be. When you seize the initiative to connect, together you will form the deep communion that marks the soul friend.

---

2. A quotation of Bishop Bardsley in Stuart and Brenda Blanch, eds., *Learning of God: Readings from Amy Carmichael* (Fort Washington, Pa.: Christian Literature Crusade, 1986), 69.

soul souvenirs

1. What dreams (big or little) have played a part in your personal adventure or Quest? How have those dreams connected you to others in meaningful relationships?

2. How has God surprised you with an adventure you would never have dreamed of (or maybe even chosen)? What gifts or grief (or both) have you encountered in the adventure?

chapter 2

coffee clouds

I had some dreams; they were clouds in my coffee.
CARLY SIMON

Like any couple, Les and I did a lot of dreaming together before we got married. We had a shared heritage, shared values, and a shared vision for our future. We even had the same name. And during our seven years of dating we certainly had ample time to dream. One of the things we decided together was to live a healthy life, which included a commitment to good food, healthy habits, and regular exercise. One of these "healthy habits" was a commitment to go coffee-free. That sounded fine to me; I'd never even tasted coffee. Growing up in the age of percolators and church coffee in fellowship-sized urns, I had never felt its enticement.

We got married shortly after graduating from our university, and moved from our Midwestern roots to the West Coast, locating in Pasadena for graduate school. I quickly got a job on campus, and as the most recent hire I inherited the hospitality tasks, including making the coffee. But this West Coast coffee was like nothing I had been exposed to before. I was instructed to buy fresh-roasted coffee beans at a little roaster down the street, as well as vanilla beans to add to the mix, which would infuse the beans with even more flavor. And I was admonished to do some taste testing to make sure the results were of the best quality. Furthermore, I was to keep the coffee flowing all day. I quickly discovered coffee was a valued commodity to most of my colleagues, and its making could be elevated to an art. Intrigued, I began to drink it now and again at work.

Soon I became a coffee enthusiast, wholeheartedly embracing this warm, wonderful, energy-boosting drink. There was just one little hitch. Les. And our shared vision of a healthy lifestyle that had now become nothing more than clouds in my coffee. While it didn't please Les, who called my new favorite drink "Satan's syrup" just to razz me, I thank God that he was eventually able to graciously concede and allow me this diversion from our dream.

Letting go of dreams that have been a script to our quest for happily-ever-after is no easy task. Even the little details of our imagined bliss can become monumental disappointments to us. One of the myths we hold deeply is that if we love someone we will always feel the same way about things. I tell Les today that God was just preparing me to live in Seattle, where coffee is as central to the culture as clouds are (and I fit in nicely with my daily triple-shot latte). We recently celebrated our thirtieth anniversary, and with three decades of marriage behind us, it's hard to imagine that something as incidental as drinking coffee could have threatened to create a rift. But every union contains plenty of potential catalysts for division.

More recently it's not the coffee that has been the issue, but the cost. When Les opened our mail, he took a red Sharpie to the latest Visa bill, circled each and every Starbucks charge over the course of the month, and placed it front and center on my desk with a yellow sticky note simply asking, "Really?" To my mind each and every one of those charges was justified. Scanning the bill, I could see the faces of those I met with over warm cups of coffee. My weekly moms' group; the college girls from church I signed up to mentor; the friends who shared cathartic moments of laughter or the ones who shed tears; the biweekly breakfast meetings over oatmeal and coffee with my mom and aunt. I see the quick drive-through stops with a carload of hungry boys after school, and the drinks that got me through long writing sessions for a recent deadline. Les, meanwhile, sees an inordinate amount of money being invested in a relatively luxurious and completely optional commodity.

No matter how deep the synchronicity of souls, there will always be gaps. True love wakes up every morning and recognizes the need to stretch stiff muscles that may even be sore from the work of loving the day before. We have to warm up our generosity of spirit and stretch into grace. We have to willingly take on the work of loving and being loved, giving it everything we've got. Happily *ever* comes only *after* you decide that loving *is* your quest, and that means stepping into life with someone whose view of coffee and costs and even clouds might be very different from your own.

soul souvenirs

1. When have you had to relinquish a part of your dream on your quest for happiness when you realized someone you love didn't share it? How did that experience impact you?

2. When have you experienced the gift of someone stretching into grace, relinquishing a dream for your sake? How did that make you feel, and what have you learned from it?

chapter 3

flying wishes

"We are all going on an expedition," said Christopher Robin.   A. A. MILNE, *WINNIE-THE-POOH*

We are questers, all of us. Hearts open and expectant, seeking and searching. Longings as unique as our thumbprints propel us forward as we pursue relationships, make commitments, prepare for careers, and create families. Moments of blind faith when we say, "I do"; moments of back-breaking work when we walk the floors all night with a crying baby; moments of risk when we step into roles that define us in new ways in halls of learning, commercial towers, or hospital corridors. There are battles to be fought on the altars of our hearts, sacrifices to be made, baptisms by fire and middle-of-the-night prayer sessions, and seasons of sheer dreariness or exhaustion. The way is long and arduous, for that is the very definition of a quest.

An expedition, on the other hand, is a purposeful journey taken with a *group* of people. As Christopher Robin explains to Pooh, "That's what an expedition means. A long line of everybody."

This is why on the eve of my fiftieth birthday, at this

more-than-likely more-than-halfway point of my journey, a time when "home" is getting closer than ever, I have planned a celebration that is designed to be an invitation to expedition. Questers, all of us, walking this Jesus road of giving away all that we are no matter how small that might seem to us today. All of us needing to be reminded that our small gifts offered in faith are more than okay. That when the bread of our life is given freely to those we encounter in Jesus' name, it will be blessed and broken and become not just a meal but a heart-warming Emmaus road moment for those gathered around the table.

On this occasion we will feast at my favorite Neapolitan pizzeria around the corner from our home. There will be huge, family-style bowls of salad, and pizzas baked in an oven blessed by a priest flown over from Italy. The owner, Joe, a good Italian grandson, had his grandmother's portrait lovingly tiled onto the massive stones of the oven. Her picture is another reminder that a simple life freely given in love can transcend the boundaries of place and time, stretching across oceans and extending beyond continents and decades. When President Obama visited Seattle recently, it was Joe's Tutta Bella pizza that he requested for delivery on Air Force One. I suspect that would have made Joe's grandmother pretty proud—her family recipes being requested by the leader of the free world.

Circled around me will be my soul friends. Sandy, the adventure-loving airlift nurse, currently grounded by God's clear call to homeschool her teenage son. Melissa, the single mom of three boys, whose very presence tonight is dependent on the sheer miracle of God-ordained childcare. Margo, the adoptive mom of four beautiful multicultural children, who delivered birthday cupcakes to poverty-stricken public school classrooms, and who now runs a thriving retail cupcake business. Bonnie, a pastor whose ministry frees women from sexual slavery. Wendy, a counselor who repairs relationships and souls. Clare, a mother of two, including a daughter profoundly impacted by cerebral palsy who requires vigilant ongoing care. Kerry, a mom in her second marriage, with kids in college and kids in diapers simultaneously — whose own story of abuse has given her the courage to advocate for women and children in places of power. All of them women of strength, like Mia, mother of three, with not just one but two jobs, and Pam, the busy wife of a university president. And others besides. All of them dear to me.

And there will be an element of sparkle in this party, too, but not candles representing the flames of years past to be blown out. Instead, borrowing a European tradition for the occasion, each guest will inscribe a wish on a small square of paper. We all have them, even at age fifty; wishes hold on hard and don't let go. One of the most important things about life is the willingness to keep allowing ourselves to wish. To embrace our desires. To live with expectancy. Even in a season when life has apparently turned us away from the fulfillment of the desires of our hearts.

Once the wish is recorded, each of us will crumple that paper in the palm of our hand. But then each of us will take that crumpled wish paper and smooth it back out. Now it has texture that gives it a certain strength. We will roll it into a tube with a candle-like shape and balance it upright. Then we will take a flame and set it ablaze, watching it burn down until it disappears. This is the magic moment of surprise, as suddenly these little burnt papers begin to rise. They fly up, like shooting stars, and then unfurl and flutter back down to be recaptured by their senders.

I love these flying wish papers because they become little storytellers, narrating the arc of a quest with all its important elements of plot—from the bold moment of wish, to the apparent crumpling conflict, to the moment of surrender to the suffering of the flames, to the beauty found in ashes, and the joy received at the surprise of the story's end. And this one thing I know: no matter where we are right now on our quest, we know with certainty how the story ends, because we know its Author. That is what makes turning fifty an occasion of pure joy.

soul souvenirs

1. What dreams and desires do you have that are compelling you on a quest?

2. Who can you invite to share the adventure with you—transforming your quest into a shared expedition?

semicolon society

I did not write it. God wrote it. I merely did his dictation.   HARRIET BEECHER STOWE

One of my heroes is a saint named Hattie. A mom in her forties, Hattie was sitting in church one day, taking communion, when suddenly she had a vivid vision of an old slave being beaten to death. The vision shook her deeply, and she wept. After church she quickly walked her children home, sat down, and began to put her vision down on paper. When she ran out of paper, she kept on writing on a grocery bag. What she wrote eventually became a book, published in 1852. It was titled *Uncle Tom's Cabin*. It quickly became a runaway bestseller, outpacing sales of every book in its day except the Bible. And Hattie, who is more formally known as Harriet Beecher Stowe, became "the little woman who wrote the book that started this great war," as Abraham Lincoln himself noted.

Hattie didn't get her moving vision in some kind of spiritual vacuum. Hattie's mother died when she was just five years old, leaving Hattie and her thirteen siblings motherless. Hattie had her own share of grief, her own fill of sadness.

Still, her father saw to it that she received an education in the classics, an education which in her day was characteristically confined to males. In her twenties she joined a literary club of aspiring writers (where, coincidentally, she met her husband); they called themselves the "Semicolon Society." Don't you love that? How hip! The *semicolon*: a punctuation mark that indicates a pause that is longer than a comma yet shorter than a period. How perfectly ambiguous and completely literary. The students at Seattle Pacific University where I teach would relish a club like that.

Well, this literary hipster of the 1800s and her husband had been participating in the Underground Railroad, providing temporary housing for fugitive slaves in their home already filled with their seven children, and she had served as *anam chara* to many individuals along the way. Out of those personal shared moments with the fugitives, entering into their stories, she was able to serve as an *anam chara* in a big way, ushering an entire nation through the birth pangs of freedom and dignity for all races.

Harriet Beecher Stowe firmly believed that women had the power and the moral obligation to serve as agents of change and transformation in the world. She also believed that Christ's love was powerful enough to take on the dark, entrenched evils of slavery. Finally, she believed that she was called to play a part in that epic battle. So she opened her home to fugitive slaves, and she opened her heart to God's vision, and she opened her talents to God's purposes. Hattie's story teaches us what it looks like to pursue a long and dangerous quest, one that has the potential to change the world.

soul souvenirs

1. If you've ever felt led by the Holy Spirit to undertake a potentially difficult quest, describe the experience.

2. How has God already used your gifts and abilities and personal dreams to make a difference in the world around you? What difference might he be asking you to make next?

chapter 5

parkour
and poetry

*Anyone trying to live a spiritual life will soon dis-
cover that the most personal is the most universal,
the most hidden is the most public, and the most solitary is the most communal.*   HENRI NOUWEN

My sixteen-year-old son John loves to parkour. Parkour is a
sport that emerged from France (thus the mysterious French-
sounding name) and involves free running, climbing, and
jumping from and between buildings and walls and from posts
to poles. Any urban structure can be viewed creatively as an
"obstacle" to gracefully (and often daringly) vault or jump or
tumble over—and the more of these you can combine into
continuous movements across your environment, the more joy
the traceur (parkourer) has.

I love the running involved in parkour, and John is a strong
cross-country runner, contributing his gifts to his high school
team. But as you might imagine, the stunt side of parkour can
be challenging for moms in the faint-of-heart club (a club

membership I inherited honestly from my own mom, who is a charter member). I can't begin to understand why my son is so captivated by parkour. It's quirky and unique and something I don't really relate to, but it has paradoxically become a source of bonding for us.

I love paradoxes, things that seem on the surface to contradict each other yet somehow turn out not to. I love them because they reveal things about life that I only get small inklings of on the surface — but somehow know are hidden there, under the layers, waiting to be known by anyone who seeks. Today I am under the weather, so I find myself paradoxically feeling deep gratitude for good health. It's paradoxical that the scarcity of something is often what causes us to appreciate it more than its abundance. And so often things we think could never be congruent just are. Suffering doesn't extinguish joy, in the same way that the fulfillment of our wishes doesn't guarantee happiness. So, here it is again, the paradoxical experience of having something I don't really value at all, something I would never choose, become a priceless gift to me.

Somewhere along the way, my soft-spoken and introverted son decided to start his own YouTube channel and deliver parkour tutorials for people like him who want to learn these specialized moves. And the beauty of all of that for me is his need for a camera operator, someone to film him in action. Thus began a series of countless mother-son outings, hanging out with my son in all his favorite haunts, capturing his movements on video, listening to this quiet soul project his voice authoritatively over the urban sounds of city traffic, observing him taking the perspective of the learner and breaking each movement down into concrete, understandable nuggets. Parkour, which made no sense to me, was giving me a front-row seat from which to watch my son become a fine young man. In short—motherhood bliss. In my quest of motherhood—to know and love my son with my whole heart—parkour became the golden ticket.

As relationships deepen, they go through predictable but in some ways counterintuitive stages. Every relationship starts on the surface, in a place psychologists call "pseudo-community." This is the warm and winsome kind of friendliness that is easy to offer because the connection is based on things two people hold in common. It's relatively effortless and usually pleasant, but only so deep. We find these connections in church foyers and office cubicles and classrooms and MOPS groups.

As our time together increases, our conversations expand, and the frequency of our connections accelerate, we inevitably move into the next phase of relationship, known simply as chaos. Chaos is the phase when disagreement, disappointment, and just plain differences emerge. We don't find the joke funny, don't interpret the biblical passage the same way, don't desire the same things for our children, don't feel we've been shown the level of consideration the relationship deserves. Our tastes or pace or preferences seem to diverge. ("Parkour is not what I would choose for you to invest your time and energy. Can't you choose something worthwhile?") We just don't see things the same way. Chaos is conflict. Chaos is uncomfortable.

But here is where relationships get interesting. Because there is a mystery hidden in chaos that only the brave of heart (or the discerning of Spirit) can see. When we empty ourselves of our need to change another person (to make them more like us, or more like our fantasy for them), grace works its art, and those very quirks that were once obstacles to our affection now become the very things that endear them to us. This is the great paradox of intimacy: the things we don't want often become the ushers that escort us into the things we most desire.

Then we can enter the final and most fulfilling stage of relationship: genuine intimacy. The deepest desire of every human heart. Genuine relationship is comfortable, safe, and supportive. Because we have emptied ourselves of our need to change the other person, they now feel free in our presence to offer their very best self to us. The gift of authenticity is like no other.

And as much as we need to embrace the quirks of those we love to know them deeply, genuinely, we need to do the same for ourselves. One of my interests is poetry. When I took a poetry class as a college freshman, I fell in love with its intensity, its ability to convey feelings and ideas in a way that prose or even visual images cannot. I have too many favorite poets to count — living and dead, famous and nearly unknown. And I love *The Message* paraphrase of the Bible by Eugene Peterson because he is a poet and his expressive art is revealed on every page.

But I also enjoy *writing* poems. My poems are very personal, and sharing them is like exposing my innermost heart. There is never a time when that doesn't feel risky. In fact, whenever I decide to offer one of them openly, a part of me always advises against it. An inner voice says, "Poetry is so juvenile and clichéd," or "No one thinks of words as a real gift," or "No one will ever relate to this." But the truth remains that when I am writing poetry I am filled with joy. The joy grabs hold of my soul, and my whole being hums along in a perfect unity of purpose.

I don't know exactly why poetry seized me and has never let me go; I readily admit it's quirky. But the older I get, the more I am able to experience God's presence in those moments both of creating poems and of offering them as my gift to others. In our quest to give generously of all our talents, there are some that we might be tempted to hide away in the basement with the cautious servant. Hidden is safe — from criticism, rejection, and even growth and change. So in the spirit of the quest of self-giving, I've decided to offer up to you the first poem I ever wrote as a college freshman, mostly because it speaks simply and directly about the risk of being known. You might find it as surprising as I did that even though it's been over thirty years since I wrote it (and I've read it no more than a handful of times in all my life), as I started to write, every word came back to me by heart.

On Being Free

If I stood today,
Stripped and bare,
Of all but heart,
Left clinging there.
No structure of bones,
No drapery of skin,
No concrete image,

Just what is within.
Without woven cloak,
Of artistic design.
No additions or props,
Just heart and mind.
Would feelings and thoughts,
The essence of me,
My spirit, my substance,
Be glad to be free?
Or would I stand shaking,
Empty and breaking?
My self-image vanishing,
In dwindling dread.
My feelings of dignity,
Shrinking and dead.
I urgently long,
For truth, inwardly.
Lord, take me,
And break me,
That I might be free.

I can't begin to imagine what unexpected, eccentric (and sometimes downright bewildering) quirks you see revealed in those you love, nor do I know what secret driving passions are calling for expression within you, but I do know that even if it's parkour or poetry, the quest can only proceed if you drop your guard and open your heart, empty yourself, and welcome the uninvited gifts along your way.

soul souvenirs

1. Can you think of a time when you emptied yourself of your need to change another person (or yourself) only to discover you began to love more, not *in spite* of the quirk but *because* of it? What was that like and how did it change the dynamic of the relationship?

2. What dream-quest have you hidden because you fear it is too quirky or strange? How might God want to use that quest to help you grow and connect to him and others?

chapter 6

salon saints

> *"Do you want to stand out? Then step down. Be a servant. If you puff yourself up, you'll get the wind knocked out of you. But if you're content to simply be yourself, your life will count for plenty."*
> MATTHEW 23:11–12

We usually make the mistake of thinking that our quest will arise out of our charisma. But in my experience, those two things are often not correlated. What *does* correlate is greatness with humility. An encounter with true humility is stunning, and rare, and nearly always makes me cry. And humility doesn't come from success; it comes from suffering. Suffering, not success, is the thing that so often leads to greatness. So when I suddenly became aware that true greatness was bent over my feet, busily shaving away Chuck Taylor calluses and tidying up neglected toes, I began to cry. I knew that I was sitting in the shadow of both suffering and greatness right there in my pedicure chair.

I'd been coming here to the little family-owned shop on the corner of Elliot and Dravus for longer than I could remember. Although language stood as a barrier much of the time, these Vietnamese friends had become dear to me. Initially I was won over by their hospitality. With kindness they embraced my extremely urgent yet totally unscheduled visits. They laughed at my quirks (like ticklish feet) and complimented my endlessly boring "petal"-colored nails. I always left feeling that my soul was the thing that had truly been polished.

The atmosphere must have been contagious because, over time, a host of friends joined me in becoming regulars, and we grew dependent on our salon friends to keep us updated on one another. Like the time my friend Arlys talked her husband George into joint pedicures, and all the workers conspired to paint one of his big toes candy-apple red after he fell asleep in the chair. When George awoke to roaring laughter, they offered to remove the ridiculous red polish, but he refused. Arlys claims he still has one red toe under his steel-toed construction boots.

Eventually one of the pedicurists walked over the bridge that time and trust had built and began to open the door to his mysterious past in Vietnam. Haltingly, through the limits of shared vocabulary, Gnoc (pronounced "Knock") revealed that his father had been imprisoned because of his Catholic faith (shared by his son, a cross proudly hanging around his neck). Because his father had offered assistance to the US during the war, his family was banished to the jungle, which was considered synonymous to a death sentence by the government. Off the grid, outside of foreign awareness and aid, Gnoc had spent eight long years of his childhood with his family sleeping under shelters that were no more than branches and leaves, foraging for food, avoiding abandoned land mines and other explosives, and facing death daily. Starving, thirsty, clad in nothing but cloth from abandoned military sandbags, they roamed. Eventually he was able to get a bike and each day ride thirteen miles to a village school. Then, one fine day, his father came to the attention of a bureaucrat in the States. Back on the grid, he was awarded political refugee status. Their family was mercifully relocated to Seattle.

I wept as we gazed together at the only photograph Gnoc has of his barefooted childhood self. This singular picture, taken by an uncle and developed in Singapore (cameras and film had been outlawed in the country), was salvaged somehow from the nomadic journey of his life. His was a quest for survival and significance in the face of oppression and hostility. Yet not a hint of bitterness, not a stitch of revenge marred his spirit. Instead, Gnoc exudes gratitude for a roof over his head and grit for learning this new language and greatness in his soul as he bends humbly over feet that have never gone a day without the protective comfort of a shoe.

I had discovered that a pedicure could hold all the sacred reverence of a foot washing. Much like the one Jesus — taking a basin of water and wrapping himself in a towel — bowed and offered the disciples in the shadow of the cross. This act of gracious hospitality was the duty of the lowliest servant in any household, but Jesus used it as the ultimate symbol of grace, inviting the disciples to consider this a pattern for their connections to one another.

When the first Jesuit and Latin American priest, Pope Francis, was elected bishop of Rome, one of his first acts of leadership was a foot washing—which for the very first time in history included *women*. This was not surprising, as humility and simplicity and compassion toward the poor are the hallmarks of this pope's leadership. And regardless of religion or culture, that kind of beauty captivates the world. Greatness contained in humility is truly transformational.

Nelson Mandela was another great quester whose spiritual journey arose from the context of his place and time, and whose greatness came not from his natural charisma but from the humility and wisdom born of suffering. I had the privilege of being in South Africa one year on "Mandela Day," the occasion of his birthday in the shadow of his coming death. Everywhere I felt the impact of this man's humility. He exited prison without bitterness and offered reconciliation to his enemies, while advocating for the oppressed and restoring justice in his land. White South Africans who had been raised on apartheid wept with love for him. Black South Africans who tenderly called him Madiba, his tribal name, revered him. His humility and greatness were one and the same.

I was so moved by this experience that I penned a poem in my journal. I wrote of the beauty of Cape Town, with its remarkable Table Mountain and its beaches with wild penguins, ostrich, and baboons on the roam. I also wrote of our safari through bush country so utterly stunning in its wildlife and unique terrain. I titled the poem "Living Colors," which, of course, echoes the symbolism of the South African people reflected in their colorful flag.

Living Colors

The giant heart, Mandela,
Binding Man to Man;
The currents of two oceans,
Linking land with land.
As if the world were clasping
Shaking watery hands.
A Mountain Table—
Linen clouds,
Tuxedoed penguin guests.
Celebrate the Freedom Father.
Honor the suffering of his quest.
A light rain,
Brings a rainbow,
At first a little shy;
Then bowing brightly—
Living colors fill the sky.
She dips her toes into the sea.
Good Hope resounds,
Within me.
Onward then,
Beneath umbrella trees,
By the light of the Southern Cross.
The wind is fresh,
And smells of earth
Moon full—
Amazing in its girth.
Pride of lions, dazzle of zebra,
Journey of giraffe.

Elephants gather at the watering hole,
Drinking,
Make us laugh.
Time bends for us in Africa,
This ancient-future place.
Mythical and storied—
Beating drums and joyful dance.
Forgiveness and democracy,
Oneness in diversity.
Spirits rising,
Broken, blessed.
The unguarded beauty,
Of her people,
Embodies Africa best.

I don't think Nelson Mandela or Pope Francis would be the least bit surprised to find a saint in a corner salon. Nor would they disagree that quests often happen because of context, always hang on the hook of humility, and often lay the groundwork for our calling.

soul souvenirs

1. How has the context of your life—the place, people, and circumstances around you—shaped your personal quest?

2. How has a recent experience with suffering impacted you—for good or ill? How did it change you?

chapter 7

grace and grit

> *Keep your eyes on me, not only for direction but also*
> *for empowerment. I never lead you to do something*
> *without equipping you for the task.*
>
> SARAH YOUNG, *JESUS CALLING*

My favorite movie is Ingrid Bergman's "golden era" film, *The Inn of the Sixth Happiness*. It's the true story of Gladys Aylward, whose Jesus journey took her to China, where she won the hearts of the people, shared the love of Christ, adopted hundreds of orphans, and led them on a daring trek to safety during a Japanese invasion. All this from a woman who failed missionary training school, was told she wasn't smart enough to learn the Chinese language, and was rejected as a missionary candidate.

As a teenager living in London in the early 1900s, Gladys was short and dark-haired but longed to be what she perceived as the ideal beauty: tall and blonde. But a story she read about China lodged itself into her heart, and from that moment forward, she knew she must go there. Years later, she had saved just enough money working as a maid for her ticket on the Trans-Siberian Railway. When she heard about Jeannie Lawson, an aging missionary in China who needed help, she took that as her quest. Gladys embarked on the journey of a lifetime, enduring a thirty-mile walk in the snow and barely escaping Soviet war-zone dangers. Without language skills or the protective covering of an agency, she arrived in China only to discover it would be another two-day mule ride into the mountains to find the seventy-three-year-old Lawson. But find her she did, and together they restored an old shack and opened an inn for mule drivers.

Villagers were afraid of these two "foreign devils" who restored the old "haunted" house. But eventually their flea-free beds and amazing Bible stories delivered with delicious food won the hearts of the weary travelers, and the hotel began to thrive.

Tragedy struck when Jeannie fell from the inn's second-story balcony and died, leaving Gladys alone and unable to pay the bills. God's provision came in the most surprising way. The town governor asked Gladys to become his official foot inspector, visiting nearby villages to set free the feet of Chinese girls from the painful and hobbling practice of foot binding. On her visits Gladys was also able to tell the stories of Jesus, setting hearts free as well. When riots broke out in the town prison, Gladys was called in to restore order, which she did, thereafter visiting the prison daily and bringing reforms that made living conditions bearable. Her work in the village earned her the affectionate name Ai-weh-deh, which literally means "Virtuous One." As another sign of her commitment to the Chinese people, Gladys even became a Chinese citizen.

But Gladys had only just begun her quest. Over time she began to "buy" unwanted children, until almost one hundred of them had come into her care. When the raging Japanese-Chinese war finally reached their remote mountain village, Gladys hid her children in caves and later led them on foot over the mountains in a daring *Sound of Music*–type escape.

God had given Gladys everything she needed to serve her beloved China. With her short stature and dark features, she blended in with the people he had given her to love. Even though she didn't get her girlish wish to be tall and blonde, what she got was the fulfillment of her heart's deepest desires.

I marvel at the paradox that even our very hairs are numbered by God (be they short or long, dark or fair), and yet we can find ourselves hiding in caves under fire even while we are carrying out the very will of the One whose love-quest we have assented to. Encounters with God do not insulate us from encounters with suffering. This is why we all need an occasional infusion of grace and grit. Grace is the gift from God freely offered that assures us he cannot be hemmed in by our flaws or failures. And grit flows from the assurance that our bedrock is God's promise that his presence will go with us, and he will see our journey to the end.

soul souvenirs

1. When have you experienced God's grace and provision even in the face of apparent personal failure? How did your experience teach you something about God's faithfulness and grace?

2. What quest is God placing on your heart right now? In what ways will it require courage and grit?

wedged bear

> *"Then would you read a Sustaining Book, such as would help and comfort a Wedged Bear in Great Tightness?"*   A. A. MILNE, *WINNIE-THE-POOH*

My dense urban neighborhood in downtown Seattle is a far cry from A. A. Milne's Hundred Acre Wood, which is, of course, the cozy haunt of the beloved cast of characters who roam and play with Christopher Robin. Never mind. I am disarmed by the sheer charm and authenticity of these fictional friends. They have helped me to understand on a profound level the way God nudges me forward on this quest called life.

On one level, each Milne character is completely relatable. Like Piglet, I am often overwhelmed with my own smallness in the face of life's challenges. I recently had the privilege of giving a talk to an amazing group of women gathered in Washington, DC, who serve as advocates lobbying for the rights of women and children around the world. Deeply moved by their mission, I wanted to serve them well. After nearly twenty hours of preparation (for a one-hour plenary), I was still searching for words through the night—only hours before I had to speak.

Encounters with my own limitations cause my insecurities to resurface time and again, dwarfing my soul.

Sometimes (more often than I'd like to admit) I can identify with Rabbit, who is busy about his own purposes and miffed at the continual interruptions of his friends and relations. My then nine-year-old son, Jackson, rushes into the kitchen carrying a plastic wand, a trick coin, and a deck of Svengali cards. I am seated in front of my small desk that houses my laptop computer, catching up on my cluttered email inbox, when he blurts out, "Mommy, can I show you my new magic trick?" His question hangs in the air with excitement, vulnerability, and the sheer joy of fresh mastery. Before I can help myself, my response is, "Just a minute, Jackson; let me finish this email first." All the while I am subconsciously aware that the days are fleeting and finite and I have just missed out on one of those moments that I would have reflected on longingly in the twilight of my life.

Which brings me to the part of me that can relate so well to gloomy Eeyore. And of course I could go on and on, finding bits and pieces of myself in Roo and Tigger and the rest. But in the end, the character I relate to most is Winnie-the-Pooh.

Like Pooh, I would describe myself as earnest, affectionate, and mostly well-meaning. All good qualities, really, or at least quite innocuous. Although Pooh is a "Silly old Bear"—which means he is a bear of "Very Little Brain"—he endears himself through the generosity of his heart. If his brain is a bit "fluffy," there is one clear thought in his head: honey. Pooh wobbles around the Hundred Acre Wood distracted by an endless quest for that viscous amber fluid, nectar of the flowers, to quench his cravings. This quest, although flowing from the most natural of desires for a bear, becomes the catalyst for a great many of his misadventures. Likewise, all too often, I wobble around the woods of my life on my own continual quest for "honey" (and, truth be told, so do you).

Much like Winnie-the-Pooh, I have some gaps in my understanding, shallow pools of thought where deeper waters of knowing are called for. The wisdom of Proverbs tells us, "Knowing what is right is like deep water in the heart; a wise person draws from the well within" (Proverbs 20:5). Yet none of us knows ourselves perfectly. It is nearly impossible for us to accurately assess our own inner self, with its complex blind spots and hidden corners (although, thankfully, we can rest in the certainty that we are completely known and understood by God).

As best I can understand, that euphoric feeling that comes from words of affirmation or unbridled affection is for me what honey is for Pooh. Affirmation and affection are the sweet nectar I crave; my appetite for approval, voracious. I can quickly get lost in the woods of my life, following down paths of external affirmation rather than listening for the voice of inner purpose. I mean no harm, really, and yet there it is.

And this is precisely why I can immediately project myself into the tight place Winnie-the-Pooh finds himself as he attempts to exit the doorway of Rabbit's house following a generous meal of honey and sweetened milk that has enlarged his already "stout" midsection. He can go neither out nor back in, and is very definitely stuck.

I, too, often feel jammed into doorways, wedged in "Great Tightness" on my own personal quest for affirmation and affection. Wanting to please too many people, for instance, I have made more promises than I can possibly deliver on, thus leaving those who are counting on me at a loss. Even now I am thinking of a student I eagerly encouraged, who stayed late after class hoping to schedule a coffee to talk about her relationship questions. She recently sent me a third email, and I still haven't been able to reply with available time. I should have known better than to encourage this meeting now, in the midst of two international trips and overwhelming deadlines and family obligations. Nevertheless, here I am. Struggling to move forward, unable to back out. Again and again I find myself not only immobilized by my sheer lack of spiritual nimbleness but humiliatingly blocking the movement of those around me (like my dear student in need of good counsel). I imagine those I love trying to function normally around my stuckness, finding creative uses for me in the meantime — like Rabbit turning Pooh's south side into a towel hook.

The moment we discover ourselves wedged into a place of Great Tightness, there is nothing left to do but call for help.

Naturally, it is decided in the story "In Which Pooh Goes Visiting and Finds Himself in a Tight Place," that his friends must seek Christopher Robin for help. Rabbit goes to find him. And Christopher answers the desperate summons with those dear, familiar words, "Silly old Bear." Instantly we find Pooh's ridiculous predicament has not separated him from the affections of his good friend, but paradoxically has struck a deep chord of compassion and endearment, and above all a willing presence.

I recently encountered that same intimate, affectionate,

willing presence in the book of Hebrews, where I read: "We don't have a priest who is out of touch with our reality. He's been through weakness and testing, experienced it all—all but the sin. So let's walk right up to him and get what he is so ready to give. Take the mercy, accept the help" (Hebrews 4:15–16).

Is there a way out of this tight place? A way forward? Hope surges in Pooh and in Rabbit and all the friends and relations in the forest too. Understandably Pooh is upset when he discovers the solution will require waiting for a week for him to become "thin" again. A tear rolls down his silly, sad, little cheek.

I can relate to Pooh's tears. One day it occurred to me that almost every time I pray, I cry. And like Pooh, I think mostly the tears come from those moments of deeper awareness that who I am is not who I wish to be and that the process of becoming, of genuine spiritual transformation, is much slower and more imperceptible than I ever would have wished for or dreamed possible.

But the crux of the story for me is here, where Pooh gives voice to my heart's cry, saying, "Then would you read a Sustaining Book, such as would help and comfort a Wedged Bear in Great Tightness." Comfort and sustaining. Oh, the grace! While Pooh could not have the honey he craved (and that had gotten him stuck), what he could have was true nourishment and genuine comfort. Of course, Christopher Robin does read Pooh just such a book, which is the only nourishment Pooh has for the week, and as he listens and waits, he grows slenderer and slenderer still (now there's a diet that might work for me!) until at last all the animals of the forest band together and pull and pull until finally, and only after great effort, with a "pop," the stuckness is overcome and Pooh gains his freedom.

I think of John the Baptist, who like Pooh (what an unlikely comparison) sustained his strength on wild honey. When John's followers were upset that Jesus was getting all the attention, John embodied a paradoxical kind of spiritual stoutness. He declared of Jesus: "He must increase, but I must decrease" (John 3:30 ESV). Talk about deep soul-wells. Talk about a life determined by the inner voice of purpose. Talk about knowing the ultimate end of his quest.

I love this story of "When Pooh Goes Visiting" because everything about it rings true. It is in the Tight Places of my life that I find myself understanding at a level deeper than ever before that the way forward, into freedom, into the "Hundred Acre Wood" of God's kingdom, will be a shared one. Spiritual nimbleness will come for me only as I allow myself to be surrounded by those who will stay beside me whenever and wherever I am stuck, gladly sharing with me from the Sustaining Book. Those "friends and relations" who graciously allow time to pass as hidden transformations occur within me and who, at exactly the right time, band together and push me through the doorways of my life with all their strength. And of course it goes without saying, those who allow me the privilege of doing the same for them.

Colossians 1:19–20 tells us, "So spacious is he, so roomy, that everything of God finds its proper place in him without crowding. Not only that, but all the broken and dislocated pieces of the universe — people and things, animals and atoms — get properly fixed and fit together in vibrant harmonies." Yes!

soul souvenirs

1. Is there a character in the Hundred Acre Wood to whom you relate? Why?

2. Has a misguided quest ever gotten you stuck? What brought you encouragement and support during that time?

part two
calling

The invitation to this life of grace, this new belonging in the kingdom of God, opens the door of the heart to nudges of the Spirit within. A strong conviction builds within us that God is calling us toward a course of action that will embody his presence and fulfill his purposes in the world. As one of my pastor friends in Seattle says, "God ordains time and place." Amen. Stepping into this call is guaranteed to require a new level of humility, self-awareness, and dependency on God that stretches us beyond our capacity, requiring support and sustenance from our soul friends along the way.

chapter 9

coming clean

"Hallo, are you stuck?" he asked.
"N-no," said Pooh carelessly. "Just resting and
thinking and humming to myself."

A. A. MILNE, WINNIE-THE-POOH

A few years ago we made a surprising move with our boys from our cozy family home nestled in a neighborhood cul-de-sac to the seventeenth floor of an apartment in downtown Seattle. The Space Needle looms large outside our window, and so do the busy city streets. Even for a quirky and progressive city like Seattle, raising a family downtown is an out-of-the-box choice. Still my husband and I feel irrepressibly drawn here. And more than that, we sense a deep confirmation of God's *ordination*. A mysterious inward impression that for reasons beyond and beneath our personal affinities and whims, he wants us here, now, in this time, in this place.

And so in this place we have followed our hearts into urban projects, such as the Denny Park Commission. This eclectic group (to say the least!) took on an overgrown patch of rhododendron bushes large enough to shelter criminal activities of every stripe imaginable; pruned back the camouflage; replaced it with bright, revealing lampposts; installed ziplines and a merry-go-round. And in the spring, we brought the poetry of Wordsworth's "host of golden daffodils" to the park.

One of the realities of the move *into* the city is a daily commute with the boys *out* of the city, to a Christian school housed on the campus of CRISTA Ministries. CRISTA, a unique family of ministries housed in a former tuberculosis hospital, includes a senior living community (where my mom lives) and outreaches that encompass everything from global development to veterinary missions to a popular contemporary radio station.

Every day we frantically rush out the door to make the significant commute to school, so busily distracted with a review of spelling words, memory verses, chapter summaries, and unfolding social dramas (who did Jackson make laugh at the third-grade lunch table yesterday and how, and what happened to the eighth-grade boy who "pants-ed" a dozen seventh graders at the junior high?) that we barely notice the scenery outside our windows other than the flash of brake lights or the red or green signals slowing or speeding us on. Consumed with the world inside our car, I find it very easy to remain emotionally disconnected from our surroundings. Day layered on day, year layered on year, as we traveled north and south on Aurora Avenue, past old familiar haunts, without giving more than a passing thought to them.

My life was intensely busy, with motherhood being my prime vocation, followed by teaching at the university, and writing and travel and board work and community involvement in my city neighborhood, and the caring for family and friends. Are not all of our lives intensely busy?

But really, if you lived in my city, and especially if you loved Jesus, you might be amazed that I could drive these streets *four* times a day, *five* days a week without being literally *undone* by the human needs they reveal. Prostitution, addiction, homelessness, and poverty. Precarious living in weekly rentals. All there. Mingled, of course, with thriving retail and small establishments (with foods intriguingly unfamiliar) sparkling like foreign jewels amongst the predictable chains.

I remember one day I read about a family who moved to Seattle from the Midwest to serve as missionaries on Aurora Avenue. At first I felt dismissive and maybe even a bit defensive for my city. And then I felt stunned as I realized how much I (with my blindness and busyness) was the very reason they had needed to come. And isn't that the way it often is? Clarity comes for those who operate from outside of the culture and who can view it with relative objectivity.

Sometimes it's hard to admit that you are stuck. It's embarrassing. Depressing. Temptation can be great to engage in some form of socially appropriate rationalization, explaining away your true condition with pleasantries. But for us, as for Pooh in the story from the previous chapter, the pain will finally force us to come clean. But not before a great deal of fancy-footwork denial.

When Pooh finds himself stuck, he stretches a paw out to Rabbit, who pulls and pulls and pulls...

"Ow!" cried Pooh. "You're hurting!"

"The fact is," said Rabbit, "you're stuck."

"It all comes," said Pooh crossly, "of not having front doors big enough."[3]

What I love about Pooh is that instead of just owning the obvious, he circles around it once again, this time blaming it on the smallish door that Rabbit has placed on his hole rather than on the generous jar of honey he has indulged in. Oh, how I can relate to the layers of defensiveness that disguise my truest self!

Defensiveness. That reflexive tendency to constantly protect ourselves from criticism, from the exposure of our shortcomings for all the world to see. Of course, there are healthy ways to cope with the anxiety of not being perfect. Humor is one of the best. It gives us the grace we need to extend to ourselves and cultivates the ability to cope with our flaws and failures honestly, owning the folly of our ways.

Jesus had a lock on humor, using the nonsense image of the man pointing out the splinter in the eye of another while the log is lodged in his own wounded eye. This is not meaningless nonsense but disarmingly brilliant and meaningful nonsense. Jesus also must have had a deep understanding of the human tendency toward projection (what Pooh did when he blamed his problem on Rabbit's small door and large honey jar instead of his own overly indulgent appetite). Soul friends have the ability to communicate a love so safe we shed our

---

3. A. A. Milne, *The Complete Tales of Winnie-the-Pooh* (New York: Dutton, 1994), 28.

defenses and bare our honey-indulged selves. But nothing is as 𝕏
powerful as the Holy Spirit's work to shed light on the truth
in a way that does not produce shame and regret, only freedom
and transformation.

Much like that Silly old Bear, Pooh, when it came to my
Seattle surroundings, I wasn't just "resting and thinking and
humming to myself." I was really stuck, and someone had to
become my "Rabbit" calling out the truth of it to me. And so
slowly—where previously there had been day layered on day,
year layered on year of sightlessness—I began to see. Awareness of a new calling most often comes to me slowly, and in
phases.

soul souvenirs

1. When have you discovered that you were in denial
   about an important calling in your life?

2. How did the awareness of that calling come to you?
   Was it all at once or in phases?

chapter 10

walking trees

*Some people brought a sightless man and begged
Jesus to give him a healing touch. Taking him by the
hand, he led him out of the village. He put spit in the
man's eyes, laid hands on him, and asked, "Do you
see anything?"*   MARK 8:22

I love the story of the healing of the blind man in Bethsaida.
After Jesus smeared his spit in the man's eyes, laid hands on
him, and asked, "Do you see anything?" the man looked around
and said, "I see men. They look like walking trees." So Jesus
laid hands on his eyes again. Then the man looked hard and
realized he had recovered perfect sight.

Before you feel offended by Jesus putting spit in the blind
man's face, let me tell you how I read it. For me, the intimacy
of spit is the mark of tender, motherly love. As a mother I take
complete ownership for the well-being of my boys. They are
at the center of my attention (well, most of the time). And
they are the only living beings on the face of the planet I will
spit-clean if necessary. I don't think twice about taming John's
wild sleep-induced cowlick of hair with the moistened palm

of my hand, or using a saliva-moistened thumb-lick to wipe the sticky maple trail off the corner of Jackson's cheek after he eats French toast.

After the initial spit-clean, Jesus asked the blind man the important question: "Do you see anything?" The man looked around. He didn't do anything to cause the healing, but he did have to participate in the miracle; he had to look, to attend, to become mindful. He had to use those formerly sightless eyes. And I love his answer. He is so totally honest. "I see men. They look like walking trees."

Sometimes I think I shouldn't be completely honest. I mean, after Jesus touches me, tends to me lovingly, mother-like, shouldn't I just claim to see, even if I know I really can't see with clarity? Maybe the problem is all me. And if so, maybe I should pretend not to have it. To say, "Yes, Jesus, I see men." It's true — sort of. And yet this man knows somehow that he can be completely candid with Jesus. Totally authentic. No pretense, no false humility. "They look like walking trees."

And so Jesus laid his hands on him *again*. He wasn't angry. He wasn't judgmental. He wasn't exasperated. He was willing to touch him as many times in as many ways as it took to overshadow the darkness with his light, the blindness with his sight.

The process of seeing usually happens in stages, beginning in that place of unconscious ignorance Jesus called blindness. Oblivious to the tender miracle of God's presence or the depth of anguished suffering in the soul of someone near us — we are blind. Then inklings of something more start to tease us, and we move forward into a place of awareness. Here we begin to understand how little we have known all along. We struggle to respond and haltingly begin to act. Often it's painfully awkward, and we are full of self-doubt and, frankly, not extraordinarily helpful. But over time, as we stay the course, we gain deeper and deeper understandings until we hit our spiritual stride and develop insightful empathy and an effective response.

And in the same way that Jesus touched the blind man's eyes a second time, Jesus has reached out to me repeatedly, patiently. The spit-cleaning baptism, the seeing in my own life came in stages until there it was in perfect focus: the longings, the loneliness, the need all around me. All of it right outside my car windows, close enough to touch and feel on Aurora Avenue.

I love how the apostle Paul puts it: "our lives [are] gradually becoming brighter and more beautiful as God enters our lives and we become like him" (2 Corinthians 3:18).

When the new Community Groups catalog was dispensed at church, the group entitled "Stranger Danger" promised to gather a few people together to walk Aurora Avenue, exploring its haunts. I understood immediately that this was clearly my next step in obedience. I felt the momentum pushing me through yet another doorway. I was being called.

What a life-changing experience. To break bread together in small establishments, meet the owners, and hear their stories. To befriend the managers of the weekly hotels, know them, and seek to bless them. To connect personally with the friends who call those streets home. To meet the people embedded there, serving in humility and gentleness. God had not only spit-cleaned my sightless eyes, but he allowed me to taste, touch, hear, and smell. He was inviting me into the center, through the work of the church. On my own, I would be far too shy, but in the company of a small band of people who belong together, I become part of his body—free to roam, to learn, to serve, to see people with clarity, *men* instead of walking trees. Free to pursue a new calling.

soul souvenirs

1. When have you had the experience of finally opening your eyes to a new call—big or small—in your life? What allowed you to see it?

2. How has a church or soul friend come alongside you to help you in that call?

chapter 11

real change

*"Walk with me and work with me — watch how I
do it. Learn the unforced rhythms of grace."*
                                    MATTHEW 11:29

The landscapes that frame our lives often ground us in our
calling. When the city is your neighborhood, your life is teeming with characters. Our South Lake Union neighborhood of
downtown Seattle is largely dominated by Amazon's sprawling
campus, and is therefore populated by young, badge-wearing,
multiethnic, techies semi-affectionately known as "Amazoni-
ans." We also boast a healthy dose of otherworldly looking
biotech scientists, and more eccentrically, transients tucked
into the margins asking for spare change, competing for our
attention with cleverly phrased cardboard signs.

A few of these characters, although homeless, are not
transient. They consider these particular streets more or less a
permanent address, and we have come to know and love them
as our neighbors. Isaiah John works regular hours outside the
Whole Foods at the corner of Westlake and Denny. He is gre-
garious and sports a huge smile and a very unorthodox style.

He is also a proud vendor of a street newspaper called *Real Change*.

Vendors such as Isaiah buy the newspapers for pennies and then sell them for the list price of two dollars plus tips. The publisher of *Real Change* is a nonprofit organization that had a vision to become a hand *up* (in contrast to a hand*out*) for the homeless community. They recognized that friendly newspaper transactions could build relationships between vendor and customer, affirming the self-worth of the vendor and dispelling the customer's fears of the homeless. By meeting people where they are, *Real Change* helps homeless men and women address their immediate needs for survival while also building a more caring community.

Isaiah John is a charismatic salesman. In costumes he cobbles together from the dollar store, he takes on personas that fit the current zeitgeist of the city (currently Super Bowl mania for Seattle's prouder-than-ever Seahawks fans). Taking a familiar tune, he invents lyrics to fit the mood. He serenades passersby so effectively that he draws them into his circle for tips and sales.

Over time, Isaiah and I have become friends. Initially we shared laughter and daily updates over paper purchases. Eventually we connected at a deeper level, as Isaiah began to trust me with art sketches and journal entries in his travel log. Isaiah dreams of being a famous musician someday. But he also has a knockout comic strip idea and a book in the works. I've loved engaging with his art and offered to help him with it in every way I can through connections or opportunities. But for one reason or another, Isaiah never follows through on these offers.

I have come to know fragments of his story. Alcoholism ran rampant in his family. Somewhere, there is a mama who loves him, but for years he's been on the mean streets in many different states. When he heard Seattle was a good place, he migrated on foot. But despite his charisma, talent, and the seeds of greatness in his sketches and journals and original music, he just never quite takes the next step.

Isaiah confounds me at times. But Jeff, our friend who directs the Union Gospel Mission, a shelter in Seattle, has reminded me on numerous occasions that connecting with people whose lives are messy is not for the impatient or faint of heart. There is no formulaic relationship with direct results. I remember hearing a gifted teacher talk about her relationship to her students, each child at a different place on the spectrum of understanding. Her countenance had a glow to it as she said she had learned to meet each and every student right where they were and simply invite them to *more*. So following her lead, I have tried to keep my encounters with Isaiah simple, to meet him unconditionally wherever he is but to continue to hold out a warm invitation to more.

One day as Isaiah and I were talking, to my surprise and delight, he told me he wanted to be baptized. Jesus had always been a part of our thread of conversation, but this would be a bold step for him. Though I knew he was completely sincere, I wasn't sure exactly what baptism meant to him. Thankfully he was familiar with my church, where he had often shared community meals or picked up pantry items, and felt a sense of comfort. Because it's located on the edges of Green Lake (a beautiful little lake park dropped smack-dab in the middle of the city, as much a refuge for Seattle as Central Park is for New York), we hold summertime baptisms there. I was able to share with Isaiah that my own son John had been baptized in the lake, a wonderfully sacred and intimate experience.

Because we were leaving on an international trip the very next day, I said a prayer, sent an email to our pastoral staff with Isaiah's email address which he checks periodically from the public library, and hoped against hope that grace would pave the way.

I awakened early the first Sunday morning after our return from Africa. Disoriented from time-zone-hopping and exhausted from endless hours of flying, I checked my email. Pastor Jack, an associate at my church, wrote simply, "Isaiah John is getting baptized today, and since he doesn't have any family to join him, he is hoping your family can be there to share the moment." Instant joy! Our excited family pulled ourselves together, wrapped up a Bible for Isaiah along with a copy of *Jesus Calling*, and found our way to the lakeshore, accompanied by our dog, Charlie. Pastor Jack told us that Isaiah had come to the classes to prepare for his baptism, had been a part of Sunday worship (sitting in the front row), and was very sincere in his desire to be baptized.

Scanning the little crowd of family and friends, we could find no sign of Isaiah. We were all fully aware that due to his transient circumstances and a lifestyle that demands full attention to the present to survive every given moment, something like this, requiring commitment and intention, was a stretch. We prayed and waited. We hoped and prayed some more. We joined in the celebration as the ceremony began. One by one, followers of Christ waded into the cool waters of the lake on a drizzly August day, celebrating a holy moment on their Jesus journey.

As we neared the end of the service, Isaiah came riding up to the shore, tossed his rusty bike to the ground, and raced into the waters. I wondered if he had a warm towel or a change of clothes like everyone else did; my jet lag had left me unable to be mindful and prepared, and I regretted that. Pastor Jack gave him time to share, and his testimony was simple and sweet. They shared a warm embrace of fellowship, and in the name of the Father, Son, and Holy Spirit, Isaiah John was raised up out of the waters of Green Lake to new life. In typical Isaiah pageantry, he burst into song. It was beautiful and jovial.

Afterward Isaiah shared with us how he wanted God to help him achieve success as an artist so he could bring God glory. I knew that wasn't how it worked. I hoped Isaiah wasn't thinking of this as a golden ticket to the Grammies. But I gave all of that, along with Isaiah's complex history, over to God and asked him to be Isaiah's path to real change.

Isaiah John has taught me a lot about my calling. So much of my purpose has to do with proximity. I am a firm believer that God ordains time and place. Like the story Jesus told us about the Good Samaritan, the simple fact of Isaiah's presence in the places I call home makes him my neighbor and therefore a part of my call. Though it's hard for me to admit it, this calling hasn't always been easy.

Each time I step outside the door of my city apartment I need to plan for time to chat with Isaiah, and I need to gather up the lost coins and spare bills from my pockets in anticipation of a paper purchase. He usually has a new song he has composed that he wants to sing for me (for tips, of course), and receiving this gift takes time. Time is my most valuable resource, and there are days when I just don't have time to spare. Sometimes, when I am really pressed, I get tempted to take a hidden route, where I won't have to encounter Isaiah. And I am not proud to admit that more than a few times I actually have.

Recently, when I was ready to sneak down the elevator and avoid my daily encounter with Isaiah, the Holy Spirit intervened. Out of the blue (or out of the Spirit's prompting?), a famous study done at Princeton Seminary suddenly came back to me in clear detail. In the study an actor, slumped over in an alleyway, was placed along the path of students who had been asked to give an impromptu talk (half of them on the story of the Good Samaritan). Some were told they were already late, and they would need to hurry. Others were told to go now, but if they left immediately they would easily be on time. Interestingly only 10 percent of the students who were told they were in a hurry stopped to help *even when they were going to give a sermon on the Good Samaritan.*

It's easy to judge those students. To marvel at how little connection existed between their learning and their living. When interviewers talked with them later, they found these students had actually experienced a lot of inner conflict about *not* helping. But because they felt the urgent need to be someplace else, they just didn't stop. They were not indifferent to the suffering, nor so calloused they didn't even notice it. And so it turns out that *hurry* (not their values, faith, or good or bad intentions) was the single greatest predictor of their behavior—and mine.

One of my favorite writers, Henri Nouwen, has said that so many of us are suffering from Attention Deficit Disorder of the Soul. We so rarely give the person we are with our full and undivided attention. And when we do, it is astonishing in its effect. I love how the little red-haired, freckle-faced Sara Grimke, an eleven-year-old character in Sue Monk Kidd's novel *The Invention of Wings*, describes the glory of being on the receiving end of another's undivided attention: "My brothers had once traced Orion, the dipper, and Ursa Major on my cheeks and forehead with charcoal connecting the bright red specks—and I hadn't minded, I'd been their whole sky for hours." Who doesn't want to be someone's *whole sky*? The rarest and best gift we have to give others is the extravagant focus of our full attention. The kind of attention that it takes not just to glance another's way but to stop and stay long enough to identify the constellations that are visible in the darkness of our souls.

Nouwen didn't just observe this; he backed it up with his life. A busy and successful professor of divinity at Yale, prolific writer, and priest, he began to tire of his hectic existence and responded to an inner call to a deep life change. And so he accepted an assignment at L'Arche, a residential community in Ontario, Canada, serving adults living with developmental disabilities, where he became a community pastor and a personal caregiving companion to a disabled man. Nouwen's calling was to leave a prestigious teaching post—with its complex, sometimes politicized, and high-profile demands—and instead pursue a different rhythm of life, the gift of a new pace in a new place.

So many of the spectacular moments of Jesus' ministry occur not by plan at a particular destination, but as he and the disciples are going along the way. Often these "interruptions" irritate and exasperate the disciples, who feel a sense of urgency very familiar to most of us. But Jesus embodies an unhurried presence, a Spirit-directed rhythm far removed from the hustle and bustle of life. He finds time for unscripted moments with blind men who can't navigate to him but call out loudly, some might think rudely, to get his attention as he passes by. He welcomes the playful interruptions of children, whom he gladly slows to honor, praising them as exhibit A for any who would be willing learners. He lingers with lepers, crossing cultural taboos to heal, and hanging out long enough to still be present when one returns to thank him for the transformation he has experienced. He finds time for the sick bringing him their diseases and the seekers bringing him their questions. Interruptions turn into healings and transforming conversations and history-making encounters that only happen because of the unforced rhythms of grace that shaped his every step.

Deliberately slowing my pace, I headed to the corner where I knew Isaiah would be waiting. There he greeted me warmly with a handshake and a hug before breaking into song. For this moment, he understood that he wasn't a homeless guy on my path but a neighbor whose mirth and melody could command my attention. I stood, an audience of one, allowing his performance to fill the whole Seattle sky.

soul souvenirs

1. Whom in your daily context might you identify as part of your calling?

2. What would it look like for you to slow down and create space for kindness and compassion in the fray of your busyness?

chapter 12

kingdom math

*"The smallest act of giving or receiving makes you a
true apprentice. You won't lose out on a thing."*
MATTHEW 10:42

There is something electric about being in a kitchen humming
with purpose. In one corner, my fifth-grade son Jackson waves
a sharp knife over a mountain of Brussels sprout globes as he
slices them (and we hope only them) into halves. In another,
John, my high school freshman, stands over a utility stove han-
dling a king-sized frying pan overflowing with thickly sliced
strips of bacon. I watch the beads of sweat appear on his forehead as the bacon crackles and pops, filling the room with the
scent of heaven. Nearby, boys are slicing dinner rolls, while
girls are busy coating fresh chicken breasts with a parmesan
breading. I have my hands full scrubbing and cutting russet
potatoes and praying the oversized pot will break into a rolling boil soon enough to transform them into fluffy mashed
dollops.

We are working side by side in the kitchen of New Horizons Ministry, a drop-in center in the Belltown neighborhood

dedicated to serving homeless teens in Seattle with friendship, mentoring, resources, and warm meals. My friend Amy had signed up her family to host dinner one night a month, and so it had become a cherished tradition for a few girlfriends and our sons and daughters to serve as kitchen hands.

After the frenzy of cooking, we circle up and ask God's blessing over every guest he sends our way. The food is served cafeteria-style, so our boys and girls don clean gloves and bright smiles and line up, each one with a specific job. They pour milk and juice, top oversized slices of fruit pie with whip-cream art, and fill trays with heaps of home-cooked love.

Afterward we move to the tub-sized sinks, roll up our sleeves, and tackle the towers of dirty dishes. This is where conversations unfold around dishtowel gatherings. The occasional water fight breaks out with the help of power-washing hoses. Sometimes whipped-cream wars wage out on the sidewalk, where the boys go to get a breath of fresh air and cool down.

The kitchen of New Horizons has shown me that when someone steps boldly into a personal call, it nearly always has the effect of elevating the community around them. My boys don't serve at these monthly meals out of personal conviction—they go to have fun. And the crazy thing is they have never worked harder, or stretched higher, particularly in the area of culinary skill, and yet they hardly even notice that it's happening. What they do notice is that their friends will be there and that anything can be fun when you do it together—even washing dishes.

In the meantime, their lives have become charged with

purpose and enriched with understanding as they connect with kids their own age who live on the streets of Seattle. They meet and befriend teens whose lives have imploded in ways they are just beginning to grasp.

When Amy responded to the call to commit one night a month to nourish these discouraged kids, she knew she felt called by God to do it. At first she volunteered like us, as a kitchen hand, helping a good friend. She watched and learned, honing her understanding of proportion and timing. When it came time for that dear friend to move away, she felt the tug and decided to step into the role of "lead chef." Never mind that the timing was, let's just say, "challenging." Amy had just started her own business, running a local frozen yogurt franchise called Menchies, and she has three busy children and a husband who need her support. She responded to the nudge anyway, allowing it to shape her life in the direction of a call.

Taking a deep breath, she pulled together a couple of menus for her rotation (including the ever popular "breakfast for dinner" menu), accustomed herself to the necessary Costco runs, used her advanced math skills to figure proportions, rolled up her sleeves, and dove in. She knew she wanted to include her own children, but she never imagined how profoundly it would impact us too. One obedient step — one night a month. On the one hand, something so small that it felt like a pebble of kindness in an ocean of need. On the other hand, something that required the extravagant investment of her time, talent, and money, and the teamwork of family and friends surrounding her. That one step of obedience is rippling out to shape our sons and daughters into future husbands and wives who know their way around a kitchen and are at home with a potato masher and a dishtowel. Meanwhile they are witnessing the pain of neglect which so many marginalized kids experience right here in our hometown, and learning in living color the devastating outcome of abuse and addiction..

The teenage years are so fragile. Not only does a hormonal storm rage in every adolescent body, but a brainstorm swirls in every adolescent mind. These are crucial years of development that determine the trajectory of our lives. These are the days of discovering a personal passion and developing it. Teenage brains are undergoing a massive remodeling project as the neurons prune back and line themselves up in the pathways of attention and focus. Teens are by nature extraordinarily creative and astonishingly courageous. But unless a foundation of safe attachment is laid, a set of knowing eyes that look back with love and understanding, these young men and women stay in the reactive state of vigilance, working to be safe. Fighting and fleeing become a way of life. Kids do it on the streets of Seattle, and kids do it in a million other ways within the walls of family homes.

New Horizons is giving kids whose attachments have failed a place to discover their strengths, to be seen and be safe. A place to relax and grow and become. The amazing thing, it's accomplishing that for our own kids as well. It's activating their capacity to see others with empathy, growing their self-awareness, giving them access to their own internal compass—those neuro-pathways that go directly to the heart and provide a deep sense of what is good and right and true. So often, when we respond to the call, we fear that the people in our inner circle will lose out while we focus our attention on others. But time and again I have found this doesn't prove to be the case. In the new math of the kingdom of God, when we give we receive in good measure, pressed down, shaken together, and running over.

My favorite moment of the evening is when the guests come back with full tummies and empty trays. I drink in the smiles of these not-quite-children-not-yet-adults, who for this moment in time feel safe and secure and content. And laugh at their surprise that even Brussels sprouts (with a heavy dose of bacon) can actually be delicious. Who knew that Brussels sprouts and bacon could do all of that?

soul souvenirs

1. What nudges are you feeling that might be invitations of God into a new call?

2. When and how have you experienced the ripple effects of blessing on people in your inner circle when you give away your time and talents to others?

spilling hope

*Joyfully you'll pull up buckets of water from the wells
of salvation.*   ISAIAH 12:3

When we first came to our church, Bethany Community, the whole congregation was captivated by an all-church campaign called "Spilling Hope." In partnership with a compassionate ministry working in Uganda, the church would fund and dig wells, thus "spilling hope" through the provision of close, clean water sources for our African neighbors. We know from in-depth research that bringing clean water sources to communities is the most effective strategy for combating poverty. In places of need, basic helps like water, mosquito tents, and deworming medications accomplish miracles of transformation.

In church we watched the miracle unfold via video footage of a pump spilling those first rushing streams of water. We saw the response in the faces and the voices of laughter and the limbs clapping, dancing, stamping out the vicious cycle of waterborne disease, illness, and lethargy. Breaking the chains of captivity — the all-consuming daily journeys for water from faraway sources — to free time for work and school and play.

Seeing this transformation was an infusion of hope to our hearts in Seattle.

And it spilled into every nook and cranny of our church community, all the way to my son's first-grade Sunday school class. In an effort to involve the kids in a meaningful way, the teacher had them spend some time brainstorming ways they could raise money to help pay for the wells in Uganda. Each child had to think of at least two things to write down and share with their class.

Later, doing the laundry, I discovered the folded note in Jackson's pants pocket with his list.

1. Write a book.
2. Lose a tooth.

Item one, "Write a book," was self-evident. Both his parents were writers, so really, it was a vocational path well known to him. Item two was a bit of a mystery. Lose a tooth. What on earth? How odd. I wondered what his teacher had thought when he had shared it.

That's when it hit me.

When Jackson's older brother, John, a fifth-grader at the time, lost his last tooth, I had remembered late that night that it was important for the "tooth fairy" to do her duty. The boys shared a room, and Jackson, in the prime of his tooth-losing years, would be disappointed to discover that his older brother's tooth had not produced the expected prize. Sleepily and in the dark, I grabbed a couple of bills from my husband's wallet to slip quietly under John's pillow, hoping against hope I would not be heard by either boy.

The next morning when John emerged from his room, his

eyes were wide with surprise and twinkling with mischievousness. "Mom, look what the tooth fairy left me," he said as he held up the two crisp bills side by side—a one and a *twenty*.

My heart skipped a beat. "The tooth fairy must have made a mistake," I mumbled. What kind of precedent had this crazy error set? My first-grade son had a mouth full of baby teeth, sure to cost the tooth fairy a fortune, as my husband was bound to point out.

Now, weeks later, a Sunday school class activity made it completely obvious to Jackson that the best way to earn substantial money for his offering was to lose a tooth. And I smiled wide (flashing a mouthful of very stable and permanent teeth, even those "wisdom" ones I was supposed to lose but couldn't bear to part with in the event they might possibly help me out someday). How like God to take the moment of my forgetfulness and folly and human frailty—a thing I set in motion with the potential to cause a sense of entitlement and expectation that could play out in self-interested justice between brothers— and transform it into an opportunity for my child to experience the freedom of generosity, becoming a droplet of hope.

Hadn't I recently read in Mark 4 about how the kingdom of God is like a seed thrown into the field by a farmer, who then goes to bed and completely forgets it? This is a parable I can *totally* relate to, in all of my moments of unintentionally forgotten "to do's." But the seed sprouts and grows. The man has absolutely no idea how it happens. The earth does it all without his help: first the green stem of grass, then a bud, and finally ripened grain. And when the grain is fully formed—he reaps! Harvest time. The seeds of transformation grow secretly within us all.

> Those who think they can do it on their own end up obsessed with measuring their own moral muscle but never get around to exercising it in real life. Those who trust God's action in them find that God's Spirit is in them — living and breathing God! Obsession with self in these matters is a dead end; attention to God leads us out into the open, into a spacious, free life. (Romans 8:5–6)

And here it is again, the central place of the church in the work of transformation, pulling us together for the harvest. Alone, our individual ripened grains cannot accomplish much — together, they become the bread of life, the waters of hope.

Somehow the Spilling Hope campaign must have lodged itself deeply in the soul of my boy. When Jackson was required to memorize and recite a poem for his third-grade class, he skipped by all of the usual silly choices and, entirely on his own, chose "Hope Is the Thing with Feathers" by Emily Dickinson. Morning by morning, during the daily thirty-minute drive to school, we filled up our hearts with sounds of hope.

> *Hope is the thing with feathers,*
> *That perches in the soul.*
> *And sings the tune — without the words,*
> *And never stops at all.*
> *I've seen it in the chillest land,*

And on the farthest sea.
And never,
In extremity,
It asked a crumb of me.[4]

One day I had Jackson recite the poem for Aunt Jill. Aunt Jill spends her hours serving as a chaplain at Baily Bouchay House, a hospice for those living with AIDS and suffering in the final stages of terminal illnesses. Last month alone, fifteen of the residents they tenderly cared for had died. Aunt Jill understands *extremity* like no one I know. She wades into it daily, those farthest seas. And though the poem was familiar to her (in deeper ways than ever I could have guessed), it moved her to hear it from Jackson, this fresh young soul a vessel for such old truth.

Later she recounted to me a phone conversation with one of her dearest friends, a retired hospital chaplain living in Texas, for whom the poem had held a special shared meaning. So much so that this friend had spent time exploring the poet's old homestead in Amherst, Massachusetts, and now wept to hear of how the poem had stirred a young boy's heart. And hope feathered away to Texas from Seattle, and flew back to roost in my heart. All because of a church's decision to engage in spilling hope, and did.

---

4. *The Poems of Emily Dickinson*, ed. R. W. Franklin (Cambridge, Mass.: Harvard University Press, 1999).

soul souvenirs

1. When have you witnessed God doing a great work through your life that is sheer gift, not based on anything you have been intentionally working to accomplish?

2. When has God taken a mistake you have made and redeemed it, causing it to serve as a catalyst for something good? What was the result? How does it continue to shape your faith journey?

chapter 14

three churches

> *They all realized they were in a place of holy mystery,*
> *that God was at work among them.*   Luke 7:16

Sometime after my fortieth year I stopped throwing myself birthday "parties" and started throwing birthday "projects." I love the bonding that comes from doing something meaningful with dear friends, and the conversations that unfold around shared purpose and participation. I feel bold about asking my friends to volunteer on my birthday because I know they want to give me a gift, and <u>nothing would be more special to me than the gift of time and talents invested together.</u>

This past February the birthday project was Tabitha House, the women's shelter run by my church, Bethany Community, in the Green Lake neighborhood of Seattle. The church is situated in the midst of a cozy city block that is bordered on one side by Aurora Avenue, portions of which have become a place of poverty, pain, homelessness, and addiction. On the other side it borders the busiest city park, a beautiful lake teeming with wildlife and busy rowers and rimmed with broad pathways continually hosting walkers, runners, skaters, and dogs of every shape, size, and breed. In short, a perfect place for the ministry of hospitality. A beautiful place to gather up a few of the dislocated and broken pieces of God's universe and help them find their proper place.

Because the shelter uses church spaces also needed for weekly ministries, each day a team of volunteers sets up the bedding and serves a nourishing meal to the nightly guests. On this birthday, a group of friends joined forces to give the shelter kitchen a spring cleaning, while others organized the clothes closets, making things orderly and accessible for women needing something professional to wear on a job interview or something warm to layer over their clothes on the damp and rainy Seattle streets. Yet another team tackled the food pantry and helped to restock missing items.

After these deep-cleaning projects, the whole group gathered in the early evening hours to put out the bedding. We adorned each newly arranged bed with a brightly wrapped warm scarf. Some of the creative types added a personal touch, such as lip gloss or a coffee card, to make it even more of a treat, and all of us penned a loving note to include in the package. Following nothing more than the inner nudges of our hearts, we each knelt at the foot of one of the beds and prayed for the guest who would rest there that night. Then we circled together, shared a liturgy written by the volunteer shelter chaplain, and blessed all who were to enter and all who were to serve. With full hearts, we retreated quietly, before the guests arrived (as we were not legally trained and vested volunteers). It wasn't much really. In fact, it felt a bit small, but we had given our whole selves, and had felt such great joy.

Later, as I saw this friend or that, they often commented how they had continued praying faithfully for the unknown guest they had secretly served that day. I marveled at that.

When spring arrived, my friend Arlys found herself, alongside her own small group, serving at a "Love Your Neighbor" project at Mary's Place, a day center for women and children journeying out of homelessness, run by the Church of Mary Magdalene. On that day Arlys was using her significant culinary skills (she was once featured on the cover of the swanky *Seattle* magazine as the "Martha Stewart of the Northwest") to create a special Saturday morning brunch-and-worship event.

Leaving the kitchen, Arlys surveyed the tables, silently breathing a prayer for God's direction to the place and person who most needed her. Arlys is the kind of person open to "tugs" from the Spirit. She grew up in Africa and survived the death of her father and brother on the mission field. She has a soul-well so deep that if you dropped a coin into it, no sound of it hitting bottom would ever be heard. Sorrow drills the deepest wells, and hers wasn't empty but brimming over with the living waters of God's enfolding love.

Feeling a definite tug, Arlys turned her attention to a particular table filled with seemingly disconnected individuals and unobtrusively sat down.

No one at the table engaged her in conversation, and feeling a check in her spirit she waited quietly, openly, patiently. She waited — creating a space of hospitality but not forcing her way in. Finally, after a nearby cell phone conversation ended (which she couldn't help but overhear given the proximity), Arlys sincerely complimented the guest about her motherly wisdom over the phone. With the door opened, the story unfolded about all of this woman's children, spread across the city in foster care to keep them warm and safe and well-fed, as she struggled to regain a firm footing. Concerned for her new friend, Arlys asked her where she spent her nights. The woman told her that when she could, she loved to stay at Tabitha House.

At the mention of Tabitha House, Arlys ignited with recognition and fondness, and told how deeply impressed she had been on the night we shared in the good work being done there. Astonishment in her eyes, tears rolling down her cheeks, her tablemate slowly reached into her pocket and pulled out a worn, tattered card. It was the note she had received the night my birthday friends had served there three months earlier, in gray, dreary, mid-February Seattle.

Somehow, amidst the constant moving, the endless transitions that homelessness creates, somehow even in this—she had held on to that note. Recounting the soft warmth of the scarf she had discovered on her bed, and the festive cupcakes, she smiled. Arlys had given a plum scarf, and her tablemate knew just which woman had received it, and that she still wraps it around her neck daily (even in the changing spring rains). She shared how deeply touched all twelve of the women had been that night, feeling cherished by their anonymous friends.

Holding her note, she explained to Arlys that she had asked God to give her a way to say thank you. And here, beside her, several months later, sat Arlys—in answer to her grace-filled prayer. In answer also to the whispered prayer Arlys breathed in reverently as she surveyed the space. I'm not sure who pushed whom through the doorway, but I do know that there was support, transformation, and joy all around. Both of them felt free. "Do you think anyone is going to be able to drive a wedge between us and Christ's love for us? There is no way! Not trouble, not hard times, not hatred, not hunger, not homelessness" (Romans 8:38 – 39).

It wasn't too long after the "Love Your Neighbor" event that Arlys was asked to give a "living witness" in church one Sunday. She was stunned when, in response to the story she told about finding her friend at Mary's Place, the crowd erupted into applause. This might not surprise you at your church, but Arlys goes to University Presbyterian, with its high church beauty and reverent worship. And so the gifts and the grace and the gratitude and the answered prayers spread across the Hundred Acre Wood of God's kingdom in Seattle. Connecting not just two amazing women, but two bodies of Christ — no, three. From Tabitha House at Bethany Community Church, to the Church of Mary Magdalene extending hospitality in downtown Seattle through Mary's Place, to a Presbyterian congregation worshiping in the shadow of the University of Washington.

When it comes to the work of calling, the church plays a starring role in the Hundred Acre Wood of God's kingdom. As Christ made visible the living God, the church makes Christ visible in the world through our lives of responsive obedience to our call. "At the center of all this, Christ rules the church. The church, you see, is not peripheral to the world; the world is peripheral to the church. The church is Christ's body, in which he speaks and acts, by which he fills everything with his presence" (Ephesians 1:23).

soul souvenirs

1. How does praying for someone, or serving them, create a meaningful bond? Have you experienced a bond with someone through prayer when you don't even know them?

2. When have you experienced being called into a small part of a bigger thing God was accomplishing? How did you discover the bigger picture?

chapter 15

apron prayers

*If you only look at us, you might well miss the
brightness. We carry this precious Message around
in the unadorned clay pots of our ordinary lives.*

2 CORINTHIANS 4:7

Almost three hundred years ago, a young man named John
Wesley felt his heart "strangely warmed" by a personal experience of God's grace. John and his brother, Charles, became
major players in church history when their "Holy Club" at
Oxford, England, eventually sparked what became the Meth-
odist movement (part of the great stream of church history
from which my own Nazarene heritage flows). Charles, with
his gift of music, wrote countless hymns that still shape worship today, including "And Can It Be That I Should Gain" and
"Hark! The Herald Angels Sing."

The mother of John and Charles Wesley, Susanna (actually
mother to nineteen children, ten of whom survived to adult-
hood), was much like the Bible's Lois and Eunice, who transmitted the faith to Timothy. An amazing mom, she invested
deeply in the education and faith development of her children.

She homeschooled all of them, including her girls, refusing to have the girls share in any domestic chores until they had learned how to read and write (not just in English, but also in Latin). I don't have to tell you how rare that choice was in the early 1700s. And I have to believe it would have been an amazing sacrifice not to have the domestic help of her daughters while homeschooling and serving as a pastor's wife.

A woman of singular faith, Susanna is famous for what I call her "apron-over-the-head move." Whenever in the midst of her busy daily life she felt the need to talk to God, but couldn't get quiet time away, she would simply pull her apron up over her head (a signal her children quickly learned to honor). Right then and there, in the privacy of her apron covering, she would talk to God, seeking his wisdom and direction. I think all women with deep faith must have their own version of the apron-over-the-head move.

One of the most important gifts Susanna received through her apron prayers is the gift of discernment, that amazing ability to see beneath the surface and beyond the present moment to hear and apply God's perspective to our current context. When it comes to understanding our calling as women, discernment is priceless.

My friend Mia would laugh at the comparison, but she reminds me a lot of Susanna Wesley. Along with parenting her three gifted teenage boys, she also manages to work two demanding jobs and is deeply involved in serving her church, friends, and community. In other words, she is a woman who leans into her calling with all her soul. As I have grown to know her more deeply, I have become increasingly aware that her discerning "apron prayers" infuse her activity with a quality of joy and aliveness that is rare and precious. What a gift!

Recently she sent me an apron-prayer text as I faced some new health challenges: "God, give Leslie the strength and stamina for this journey, and fill it with the sweetest reminders of your overflowing love for her and her three boys [John, Jackson, *and* Les!]. Jesus, this is your story start to finish. Every provision, doctor, nurse, miracle, tear, discomfort, comfort, grace, and healing! You are the author of our faith and hope! Thank you, Jesus, for carrying Leslie."

So often what we are called to appears so ordinary and unadorned that, save for apron prayers, we may just miss the brightness and beauty God is inviting us to. The gift of discernment, for instance, invites us to step into a calling that turns the clay pot of an ordinary text message into a masterpiece of prayerful comfort.

soul souvenirs

1. Do you have your own "apron-over-the-head" move that allows you to tap into God's wisdom and listen to his voice within the stream of daily life? How would you describe it, and when do you tend to use it?

2. When have you experienced the gift of discernment that turned something seemingly ordinary into something extraordinary? When did you experience this most recently, and how is it shaping your sense of calling?

chapter 16

stirred to action

Well-behaved women rarely make history.
LAUREL THATCHER ULRICH

As I pursue my call, there is another soul friend I am drawn to—another sister who is a traveling saint. Really she is just a girl, or at the very most a young woman. Her name is Sophie Scholl, and she was a student at the University of Munich during Hitler's rise. Passionate in her faith and belief in the dignity of all people, she joined forces with her brother Hans and a group of friends to create The White Rose, a society committed to nonviolent resistance against the Nazis. They put their ideas into six leaflets, and Sophie worked to distribute these on the university campus. On February 18, 1943, she, her brother, and a dear friend were arrested for distributing the leaflets (February 18 is my birthday, and has become a built-in time of remembrance for me about her bold faith and love). After a trial, in which she was convicted of high treason, she was executed, along with her brother and friend, just four days later, February 22. Her last words: "Such a fine, sunny day, and I have to go, but what does it matter if there are thousands of people awakened and stirred to action."

And they were. The Allied forces got hold of the leaflets and distributed them all over Germany. Sophie Scholl and The White Rose changed the course of history, playing a significant part in turning the tide on the great evil.

One of the darkest days of my life was the day I toured Dachau, the first concentration camp established in Germany. Eerie, silent, sparse, this unimaginable place is located in a little medieval village northeast of Munich, such an unlikely location for what would become a monument to immense suffering. It is estimated that nearly 26,000 Jews were executed there. Darkened as my soul was by the sight of Dachau, my husband, understanding my intense admiration for Sophie Scholl and The White Rose, hired a cab to take us to see the white bust of Sophie Scholl that honors her memory on the University of Munich campus. Such a small girl, whose faith and willing sacrifice made such a big difference.

Lately I've been drawn by God into an encounter Jesus had with a woman whose story is told in Mark 7 and Matthew 15. The story opens with Jesus traveling with his disciples in Tyre and Sidon — unusual since he didn't leave Jewish territory much during his ministry. However, because the Pharisees had become *very* unhappy with him, some savvy scholars think Jesus was so tuned in to the timing of God's unfolding plan that he had to leave the brewing storm of escalating tempers and go "off the grid" lest he rush the climax of the conflict which led him to the cross.

In reality Jesus was probably weary. The past few days had been demanding for him, beginning with the sad news that his cousin John—possibly the one person on earth who understood Jesus' calling, purpose, and identity more than any other—had been brutally murdered by the king. (John had dared to confront the king about an affair, and this bold truth-telling had eventually led to his beheading.) After receiving this difficult news, Jesus had sought an out-of-the-way place to think and pray and grieve, but somehow his location had been leaked, and a crowd followed him there. Desperate and needy people came, motivated to make the demanding journey to see, hear, and touch him. They longed to be healed and led and then, finally, miraculously, fed. Immediately following the miracle of the loaves and fishes, Jesus had gone alone farther up the mountain, seeking silence, retreat, prayer. He had prayed through the night and into the near-dawn.

Then, at around four in the morning, he had come walking on the water to the seafaring disciples. Peter stepped out of that boat, in faith, and started toward Jesus, until fear gripped Peter and he began to sink. I love the way Jesus reached out to save him in his moment of weakness, without hesitation. And yet, how weary and alone he must have felt in all of it.

And then the Pharisees had come to him—questioning, oppositional, obstinate. So he needed to get away from it all. To be in a place where the work he was called to wasn't so visible and in his face. Can't we all relate to that? I know I can't write at home, where every nook and cranny of my environment cries out about an unfinished task or a waiting chore, and the voices of my precious children call out to me in dependence and desire, if not genuine need.

So here Jesus is in Tyre and Sidon, among the people

whom Joshua had led the Israelites to conquer in numerous Old Testament battles. Surely he can retreat here, in this foreign place. Instead, a Syrophoenician woman approaches him, desperate for her daughter to be healed. She finds Jesus in his hiddenness and lays out her need.

But then the story takes a surprising turn. *Jesus seemingly ignores her.* Yet her passion intensifies. Nearly undone, the disciples ask Jesus to help them take care of her one way or another. She addresses Jesus as the Son of David. This says *everything*. She knows who he is. The Jewish leaders, whom he came to serve, are rejecting him as Messiah, and yet she gets it. She *knows*. But then he says, "It's not right to take bread out of children's mouths and throw it to dogs." Okay, did I just hear that?

Did my "love your neighbor" Jesus, the one who told me to care for the Samaritan (a similar kind of dynamic), just call this Syrophoenician woman a dog? I mean, I can understand that he feels a bit irritated by the interruption, but did he really just ignore and insult her?

I don't think so. The more I've thought about this encounter, the more I believe that what is really going on is that Jesus just entered her world in a way that she would deeply and almost instantly understand.

Jesus knew that caring for her family was the central focus of this woman's life, and the symbolic heart of that care was *the family table*—something completely familiar to her, the gathering place, the point of warmth and connection, at the core of her sphere of responsibility.

Jesus was basically saying to her, "You have your family

to care for, and I have mine. You have your daughter, and my children are the Jews. My hands are full. In this time and space continuum I am limited to right now I need to give myself to my family with an extravagant simplicity of focus."

The Syrophoenician woman is neither offended nor shut down. She understands Jesus' purpose but still finds her place within it. "Even the dogs get the scraps," she argues. Who among us hasn't experienced that indulgent moment of giving a special treat from the "table" to our overjoyed canine?

And Jesus responds, "Oh, woman, your faith is something else. What you want is what you get!" (Matthew 15:28). And just like that, her daughter is healed.

The Syrophoenician woman "got it." She understood who Jesus was and trusted his healing power. She was humble. She didn't have to be the most important person there; in fact, she was okay being the least important person there … *but* she was strong, with a moral courage that came from a commitment to alleviate suffering, to fulfill her call to mothering, to be a voice for the voiceless. She understood that mercy has ripples, and everything is connected.

Plus I picture her making her plea with a twinkle in her eye. What lightning wit and wisdom, what chutzpah — to use a perfectly apt Jewish word in describing a very non-Jewish Syrophoenician woman!

I love this woman. Her devotion as a mother fuels her bravery; her sense of humor springs from her humility; her genuine faith stands against the cultural tide; she is bright, engaging, and proactive. And the fruit of her faith is the healing of her daughter. In fact, I imagine it might have been the

Syrophoenician woman that Jesus was thinking of when he said to his own people, "If Tyre and Sidon had seen half of the powerful miracles you have seen, they would have been on their knees in a minute. At Judgment Day they'll get off easy compared to you" (Matthew 11:21).

Harvard professor and Pulitzer Prize–winning historian Laurel Thatcher Ulrich is famous for saying, "Well-behaved women rarely make history."

It's something the Syrophoenician woman and Sophie Scholl have taught me. Faith that cannot be silenced makes all the difference. I don't know what needs have found your attention, what injustice is at the forefront of your call. But I do know that faith in action, whether considered simply an annoyance or high treason, whether it costs you your pride or your life, is the kind of thing Jesus responds to by saying, "Woman, your faith is something else. What you want is what you get!" And that is the call we are invited into.

soul souvenirs

1. When have you been so moved by the suffering of another that you were stirred to action and became a persistent and powerful advocate for them? What did you do? What happened?

2. When have you experienced a kind of moral courage, humility, or playfulness that gave you the leverage to accomplish something big? How will this shape future promptings from God for you?

part three
crisis

Sometimes events unfold within us or around us that leave us hanging on to nothing more than faith, hope, and love—and sometimes even those very foundations of our spirit slip away, leaving us bereft. Suddenly life isn't what we thought it was, and the discovery is disarming. More to the point, *we are not who we thought we were, and the knowing threatens to be our undoing.* Paul was traveling at breakneck speed down the Damascus road when his life collided with Jesus. Blinded and stilled, everything he thought was true turned suddenly upside down. Peter collided with himself in the courtyard one scary night, three times denying his relationship with Jesus. When the rooster crowed, framing his shame, he realized everything he thought he could rely on within himself had failed when it counted most. He wept bitterly. Life unfolds in ways we never anticipated and evokes things in us of which we never thought we were capable. For each of us, no matter how sincere and committed we are in our efforts, life's journey holds moments of crisis.

chapter 17

windsdays

> *Hardly a life goes deep but has tragedy somewhere
> in it.*
> AMY CARMICHAEL

Our friends in the Hundred Acre Wood, like us, have days
filled with wonder and magic, and then they have days when
the winds bluster and blow. Stormy days, those days Winnie-
the-Pooh mistakenly (but oh so appropriately) calls *Windsdays*,
bring with them inner drama as well as genuine danger and the
need for help from a friend. That's what I was thinking about
this March Windsday morning, gathered around a table with
dear friends sharing our hearts and lives. Winds of change
were blowing all around us, people being dislodged from the
comfort zones of their homes, jobs, schools, churches, and even
from familiar comfort of relationship patterns with kids and
spouses which had been stable and secure for a lifetime.

When the winds begin to blow in the Hundred Acre
Wood, Piglet is busy sweeping leaves, while the "unfriendly"
bluster keeps swirling them in all directions, making his hard
work pointless. He keeps right on, determined to do his best

against the winds, tidying up his life, until eventually his small pink frame is swept up by a gust. When Pooh reaches out for him, grabbing his sweater to give him an anchor, the sweater begins to unravel until Piglet is flying aloft like a kite.

If that isn't a perfect picture of every woman I know! We hold fast to our rakes, gathering in the leaves of our wind-blown lives with all our insufficient might, until finally we have been blown off our feet, unraveled, anchored by nothing more than a small thread in the lovingly determined clenched fist of a friend who will not let us go.

Meanwhile Owl's tree has blown over, crashing to the ground. The storm has moved from the realm of threat to reality, from temporary inconvenience to life-altering circumstance. The blustery day turns into a blustery night, complete with ominous claps of thunder and other scary noises. Piglet and Pooh make it to shelter in Piglet's home, where Pooh turns upside down in the honey pot and makes himself busy "rescuing" it. And let's be honest, who of us hasn't busied ourselves rescuing a few sweet pots of honey while a storm rages within or around us?

Finally the rains are so immense that the waters begin to flow into the window of Piglet's beech tree. At last Piglet sends out a message in a bottle saying simply, "Help me (Piglet)." It's carried away on the currents and floats out of sight. And we send our messages too — the whispered prayers and the message-in-a-bottle texts. Just yesterday, I had the following bottle-prayers float to my text message inbox:

From Kerry: "Hi Leslie love your prayers for Tyler he is at WSU in the ER sick with flu and having trouble with his diabetes. Please pray. Having kids means your heart is outside of your body forever."

From Lori: "Sorry to pester everyone, but I really need your prayers. Tough day, I need prayers for protection. Can share more Wed."

And from Clare: "Leslie, I'm going to a neurosurgery appointment with Edie today. She is not doing well and is trying to find answers. Will you please pray for her surgeon and for me to be helpful? Asking Jesus to protect, and help me be a second set of ears?"

These are the bottle-message-prayers of just one ordinary Windsday.

In the A. A. Milne story, of course it's Christopher Robin who discovers Piglet's message in the bottle. He lives on a hill, and therefore out of danger, so he sends Owl to fly to Piglet to tell him rescue is on the way. Finding them, Owl says, "Be brave, little Piglet." Eventually Piglet and Pooh float on the floodwaters to the very place where Christopher Robin is waiting. Christopher Robin exclaims, "Pooh, you rescued Piglet. You are a hero."

And haven't we all found ourselves there? We don't have a clue what to do to help our friend in danger, other than to stay by their side and pray. Yet even if we are busy "rescuing" honey the whole time, God uses the simple gift of our being with them in the flood. It's called *the ministry of presence*. And it is huge, even heroic. Christopher Robin understands this, and he sets about throwing a "Hero" party for Pooh.

One of my favorite stories from the "Hundred Acre Wood" of the early church is told in Acts 12. Peter is locked up in jail under heavy guard (four squads of soldiers), as the believers in Jerusalem send out bottle-message-prayers to God for help. In response to those strenuous prayers, God sends an angel to rescue Peter. It's a rescue so amazing that Peter thinks he must be dreaming ... until he finds himself standing free on a street corner! He goes directly to the house packed with praying friends and knocks on the door. No one can begin to believe it's Peter, so he stands on the street knocking away until they finally open up and go wild with joy.

My friend Clare has a precious, medically and developmentally fragile daughter, Sara Grace. This year Sara started middle school, an anxious time for any mom, but when your child is wheelchair dependent with extreme communication challenges and has the emotional understanding of a preschool child, this transition calls for a *monumental* exercise in trust. Clare researched her options and prayed. She conducted site visits and finally made the best choice she could, founded on her inner sense of God's guidance. But when the school year started she discovered no teacher had been hired for the program, no classroom assembled. Her heart sank. Sara responded to the upheaval by scratching her own face; Clare's self-doubt and fear were so overwhelming that she became immobilized.

She sent out a bottle-message to a few of us mothers who are linked by prayers for our children. We wept and prayed with her. And we walked the grounds of that school, praying over every physical square foot. We prayed strenuously, asking God for the deepest desires of our hearts for Sara, including the bold prayer for her to make a true friend.

Everything looked bleak, but Clare trusted God and we

trusted with her. She sent Sara off to that not-yet-finished place, depending on nothing more—and nothing less—than her sense of responsive obedience to God's leading. And so when we started hearing reports about the discovery of a Christian teacher—an enthusiastic first-time hire, who was a bundle of energy—we got excited.

And then there was the day we got *the* text. At school it was Twins Day, a theme day when BFFs dress alike to celebrate friendship. And Lillian, a classmate, had brought matching graphic T-shirts and loom band bracelets for herself and Sara. Clare hadn't even known it was Twins Day. But God did. And Sara had made a true friend. An angel in a jail cell could not surpass the greatness of this miracle: a friendship formed across the boundaries of limited communication and mobility and within the hearts and souls of two beautiful young girls.

Back in the Hundred Acre Wood, the storm has passed. Eeyore, proudly believing he has found the perfect new home for Owl to replace his crashed tree, unknowingly presents him with Piglet's beech tree. Piglet, seeing instantly that the tree is really his home, but not wanting to be in any way selfish or complaining, quietly surrenders the tree to Owl in a grand gesture of private kindness. Seeing this quietly brave act of generosity, Christopher Robin promptly expands the One-Hero Party into a *Two*-Hero Party. And the kindness of friends who are willing to share all that they are and have with one another becomes a joy-filled celebration.

We all have Windsdays. As Amy Carmichael so wisely said, "Hardly a life goes deep but has tragedy somewhere in it." And as Jesus warned us, "In this world you will have trouble"

(John 16:33 NIV). There will be strong and unfriendly winds that will make a mess of our lives, occasionally crashing "trees" and flooding "homes." On those blustery days, the kindness, prayers, and simple-but-profound ministry of the presence of dear friends will be the anchor to our unraveling, the rescue to our storm.

It is the greatest privilege of living and loving to be a part of someone's Two-Hero day. And don't be surprised when the friend whose rescue you are strenuously praying for occurs, and they come knocking on your door to celebrate God's amazing, beyond-all-comprehension, wildly-more-than-you-could-have-expected rescue operation. In a way, every single time we offer our presence *and* our prayers, God has already made it a Two-Hero day by allowing our prayers to be part of his amazing presence, his sufficient rescue.

soul souvenirs

1. Recall a Windsday when you were blowing in the winds and a friend grabbed hold of you, staying present with you in the storm. How did this change things for you? How does it impact your ability to navigate the Windsdays you may be experiencing now?

2. Who is being your "hero" right now through their presence, prayers, and kindness? What kinds of amazing rescues have you witnessed? Who are you being a "hero" to these days?

chapter 18

whirling dance

Love from the center of who you are; don't fake it ...
Be good friends who love deeply. Romans 12:9 – 10

Clare was the first new friend I made when I joined our church. She's a love-from-the-center kind of friend. Bright, beautiful, and open, Clare is easy to connect with. When I discovered we had a mutual friend in a woman named Sandy, Clare was instantly vetted for me.

Clare and Dave, her husband, have a son, Josh, age fourteen, and a daughter I've already mentioned, Sara Grace. Cerebral palsy stole Sara's language skills and confines her to a wheelchair. She's eleven now, but her developmental age is closer to three. With no mobility, she requires round-the-clock care that demands continual attention and patience. The things most of us take for granted—sharing a meal, brushing our teeth, taking a bath—are incredibly taxing. A common cold for Sara can't be taken lightly and always requires a trip to the doctor. Even getting Sara into her special van, with all of its lifts and gadgets, is exhausting.

One Sunday at church, during communion, I noticed Clare slipped out early. Later, when I found her in the church foyer, she told me: "I couldn't do it today. I'm mad at God and I don't want to share a meal with him." Clare's confession followed a dedication ceremony for a new baby. The bright-and-shiny family on the platform included a new son and a beautiful older sister who twirled around the stage in her fancy church dress.

Clare, of course, was happy for that sweet family. But as she watched the beautiful little girl twirl, the joyful movement triggered a creeping sadness within her. She ached for Sara. The string of traumatizing surgeries and the failed brain shunts are only the beginning. Clare wonders most about the thoughts and feelings trapped inside of Sara that can't find their way past her damaged brain to be expressed. She can't keep from thinking how her child's world is so unknown to her and all the people who love her. She can't keep from thinking how sad even celebrating Sara's birthday can be, because Sara can't have little girls over to giggle and play a party game together. She can't help but think how life would be if Sara could twirl and dance.

Let me be clear: Clare's faith is personal, alive, and deeply rooted. But she's no poser. She's not about to fake it. That's why her surprising decision not to partake in communion was a witness to me. Her faith-life is current, in the moment, honest. She's not one to simply go through the motions. That Sunday, she and God had to come to terms. Clare wasn't just content to pray about her sadness; she needed to pray *through* her grief until she had a new sense of God's involvement in her daughter's life.

But the breakthrough didn't come. At least not quickly. Over the next few months Clare continued to pray. She poured her aching heart out to God, sometimes only with questions and tears.

One day Clare called. "Leslie, today I don't want to walk Green Lake, or have coffee at Pete's. Today I want to go to Discovery Beach together. I've got something to tell you." Clare knows this beach is one of my favorite places in the world, a place so reverent it serves as a shortcut to worship, surrounded as it is with the stunning beauty of the Pacific Ocean, Mount Rainier standing guard on the horizon, and the forest meeting up with the sand. As we sat in the winter sunshine, feeling the crisp breeze swirl around us, Clare said her grief was dissipating. God was transforming her heart. In fact, Clare confessed, "Life is still heavy and hard, but I'm finding joy again—for the first time in a long time." She told me that she was finding surprising meaning in even the toughest times with Sara.

Clare also told me that God had given her a verse: "You did it, [God]: you changed wild lament into whirling dance" (Psalm 30:11). She told me she was ready to come back to the table with God and share a meal. They'd come to terms. She might not see Sara dance or twirl, but God would change her grief into joy anyway.

Then Clare shared about a rare and deep conversation she had just had with our mutual friend, Sandy. Sandy, a nurse, had been by Clare's side during that first dark year of hospitalization and crisis for Sara. As they talked, Sandy remembered something from those early bleak days in the hospital. God had given Clare a startling vision: a vivid picture of a little girl twirling in a pretty dress. Clare had forgotten it, along with the concrete details of where they were when it happened ten years earlier. They had thought it was a promise for Sara, that God was saying someday, maybe in heaven, Sara would dance.

Sandy said to Clare, "I think God just spoke to me. He told me that little girl twirling in the pretty dress in that vision was *you*. You are the whirling dancer filled with God's joy."

As Clare shared this astounding story with me, I reminded her of the Sunday when she couldn't take communion because she was so filled with grief. "Remember what triggered it all for you that day?" I asked. "It was the little twirling girl beside her family on the platform."

In that moment, sitting on a piece of driftwood at Discovery Beach, both of us marveled at our own discovery. God had actually been sending Clare an invitation. He was inviting her to let go of her heartache, to release the deep grief, the wild lament she had borne bravely for a decade. It was time to receive the gift of God's joy in whirling dance.

soul souvenirs

1. How has a time of suffering led you into a deeper communion with God? Are you experiencing a similar communion currently with God? Why or why not?

2. How are your honest doubts and disappointments leading you to a new place of trust and joy?

chapter 19

open doors

✳ *Prayer enlarges the heart until it is capable of containing God's gift of himself. Ask and seek and your heart will grow big enough to receive him and keep him as your own.* MOTHER TERESA

Paul writes in his letter to Timothy, "The first thing I want you to do is pray. Pray every way you know how, for everyone you know" (1 Timothy 2:1). I was thinking about this word of instruction while I gazed at a unique gift from my dear friend Kathy. A few months earlier she had been diagnosed with small cell lung cancer. It was devastating, out-of-the-blue news, and her dedication to sharing the future of her nine-year-old daughter became the focal point of her will to survive. I had been honored when she trusted me on the inner circle of her prayer team, along with her husband and sisters and a handful of dear friends.

I searched the Scriptures with my whole heart to guide my intercessory prayers. One day I read several of Jesus' parables about persistent prayer (waking a neighbor at midnight with repeated knocks to ask for provisions for a weary guest; pleading your case before the judge, like the widow who finally gets her justice). Then I meditated on the words of Jesus, "Ask and it will be given to you; seek and you will find; knock and the door will be opened to you" (Matthew 7:7 NIV). So when I talked with Kathy that day, I proudly announced I was the charter member of the "Kathy's Knockers" prayer club. Being wickedly smart, quick-witted, and slightly irreverent by nature, she thoroughly enjoyed my mistaken double entendre. We both laughed till the tears streamed.

A few days later a box arrived in Seattle from her home address in Kansas. Inside I found an ostentatiously framed brass knocker. That incongruous knocker became a symbol for me of everything I loved about Kathy and her friendship. And it became a visual reminder of the invitation God gave to ask boldly and shamelessly for what we most need. Just as if I were reaching for that little brass handle Kathy had framed, I did knock on heaven's door with all the courage and capacity within me. Over her grueling four years of treatment, I found a great sense of joy and purpose in sharing her suffering by working beside her, a partner in prayer. There were seasons of extended fasting. There was the beauty of adding the prayers of my circle of Seattle friends to her circle in Kansas. The women in my small group, my moms' group, and Debbie, my weekly prayer partner in Pasadena—all of them joined the "club." And my family prayed too. The boys prayed for her every single night at tuck-in time. Les and I prayed as a couple. My mom, the most faithful intercessory pray-er I've ever known, put Kathy at the top of her list.

And Kathy gave cancer one of the best showdowns I've ever witnessed.

One of the finest moments I shared with her during those declining years was on the Snake River in Jackson Hole, Wyoming. Kathy was an adventurer, and our families shared many travel experiences over the two decades of our post-college friendship. On this trip we loaded our kids into a van, strapped her wheelchair on top, and took off for an iconic American adventure. We meandered through Yellowstone National Park with its otherworldly geysers, beginning with a midnight show by Old Faithful, which erupted upon our arrival. We then headed on into Jackson Hole. There were magical moments along the way, like peering into the huge chocolate brown eyes of a moose drinking at a roadside pool. But there were hard moments too. Kathy wasn't feeling well, and we were beginning to wonder if the work of travel was simply too much for her to bear. She was in nearly constant pain, her energy levels lower every day, and her spirits (and ours) flagging. Close to cutting the trip short and flying Kathy home early, we reluctantly decided to go ahead with a rafting expedition we had booked along the Snake River. We imagined the gift of a gentle lazy day in the warmth of the sun, basking in nature's glory, spying forest lands, and peeking at wildlife.

But when we arrived at the outfitter, we discovered there had been a misunderstanding. The gentle float trip was actually a whitewater adventure. There sat Kathy in her wheelchair, frail from a cocktail of cancer and chemo. It was absurd to even consider going, but Kathy was resolute in her desire to do just that. We could see in her face what this meant to her. And so with all the pretend calm and confidence we could muster, we wheeled her down the river path to the water's edge and loaded her into the raft. The guide carefully placed her in the middle, on the floor of the raft tucked into the safest position possible. I began to pray my most earnest prayers as off we went, paddles in hand, along with three other rafts brimming with thrill-seeking, robust, outdoorsy types. Almost immediately we picked up speed and the waters began to fly. I have never rowed or prayed so hard in all my life. By our journey's end every other raft in our company had flipped over, turning its passengers into the frigid, boulder-filled, swirling depths. Somehow, by the grace of God and the savvy of our guide, our raft stayed upright, keeping Kathy safely afloat.

Afterward she said it had been one of the best days of her life. Those waters had entered her soul, bringing life, zest, and refreshment. I'll never forget it as long as I live, this raft trip that was God's extravagant surprise to his adventurous daughter.

Kathy died just a few months later. In the end the cancer metastasized to her brain, leaving her motionless and speechless. Even so, she rode those white waters of cancer just like she rode the Snake River, every moment choosing life over death, and fight over surrender. It was April, and appropriately, during Lent, when her suffering came to an end, just days before her fiftieth birthday. I know how the story ended for her—she's in heaven, with complete resolution, resurrection joy, and resounding celebration for eternity. But from where I sat on earth, grieving for her and her thirteen-year-old motherless daughter, I was slogging through the heart of the conflict we have with disease and death.

Hebrews 11:6 reminds me that "anyone who wants to

approach God must believe both that he exists *and* that he cares enough to respond to those who seek him." Faith is, of course, believing in that caring response even when it doesn't come in the form of our request. I had signed up for Kathy to have a life of gentle expedition; God had in mind something else altogether: a white-water adventure, shooting rapids all the way to heaven.

What I found to be true in the aftermath of that assignment from God, as president of Kathy's prayer club, was that the furniture of my heart had been rearranged. Where there had formerly been a sense of entitlement for health and longevity, there was now a deep sense of awe and gratitude over the gift of each unfolding day. A cavalier enjoyment of my loved ones was replaced by a daily sense of astonishment at their presence in my life and how each moment we share together is a treasure. And where there had been an unstudied sense of self-confidence in my own agenda for life, there was now a genuinely deep understanding that God's purposes were beyond my own. As my next birthday approached, in the shadow of Kathy's death and this milestone in my own life, I wrote a poem.

Miracle Moment

I might have missed it
If I hadn't been in this certain
Frame of mind.
Mourning for my dear friend
Whose waking hours
Have been eclipsed

By cancer's deepening powers.
Here I am, now!
Alert, alive
At this corner of my life —
Aware of its hour.
Halfway (or more)
Between then & there.
On this mid-February day
Brittle, bare,
Suddenly!
A hummingbird,
Silhouette against the air,
Suspended,
As if in prayer.
On infinitely tiny wings.
Momentary miracle,
Messenger of grace,
Forever ordaining
This time & place.
God who lives,
Outside of time & season
Has me here, now —
His context, His reason.

Even though I didn't see Kathy's healing, I did see God's revealed glory. And even on my worst day, when the conflict comes to its climax, I already know how the story ends because I've become friends with the Author. With plot twists, like riding the rapids in total safety even if you are too weak to walk, he is writing a grand story, and the only genre he chooses is love.

I know my prayers for Kathy played a part in her story. But by the gift of her friendship and God's grace, they also played a part in mine. The call to persistent prayer had reshaped my heart. Like that animated image of the Grinch when he has his moment of conversion, my heart had grown bigger and more capable of containing God's gift of himself. It wasn't my performance as a persistent prayer warrior, or my perfect record as an intercessor, but it was God's gift of himself, as prayer flung open the doors, making me a welcoming place for God. That is all. And that is everything.

soul souvenirs

1. How have you experienced prayer as a calling during a time of crisis? What and for whom are you currently praying?

2. In what small or large ways have you been changed in the process of persistent prayer?

chapter 20

glassybaby

*"You're here to be light, bringing out the God-colors
in the world."*   MATTHEW 5:14

In gray, rainy Seattle a woman named Lee Rhodes has literally infused the culture with her own brand of warmth. In
1998, Lee created her first "glassybaby." She was fighting a rare
form of lung cancer (a battle that spanned seven years) while
mothering her three small children. After enduring surgery
and countless rounds of chemotherapy, Lee began searching
for a way through the cloud of fear that had settled on her soul,
and she found it through the art of glassblowing.

Glassblowing, like good coffee and rain, is part of the warp
and woof of Seattle. The city is sprinkled with glass studios
whose open doors welcome both advanced and beginning art-
ists. I've often stopped to watch the work—the liquid glass,
the glowing furnaces—and marveled at the unique way the
breath of the artist is the force behind the form.

What emerged from the heart of Lee Rhodes, as she
was working in the glass studio with the prototypes of some
"baby glasses" her boyfriend had blown, were small, smooth,

brilliantly colored, cup-shaped candleholders (or holders of anything you might wish), which she began to call "glassybabies." Their effect was singular and special, luminous. In the words of her then twelve-year-old son, "The light of a candle coming through a glassybaby generates more: it gives warmth to a cold day, a calm token of peace in a busy world." For Lee they were the "deep breath that we often forget to take." And for the rest of the Seattle community, they quickly became ambassadors of warmth and peace.

In 2003, after working mainly out of her own garage, Lee opened her first glassybaby retail store. Lee was told there was no hope for them to succeed: nobody could ever run a successful company based simply on one product. Yet today, in the Madrona neighborhood of Seattle (just one of their three retail locations), a team of dedicated glassblowers produces about five hundred glassybaby candleholders daily, with a large percentage of the profits dedicated to funding a variety of cancer charities. After catching the eye of Martha Stewart, who invited Lee to be a guest on her television show, the enthusiasm quickly spread nationwide.

When my dear friend Kathy died of lung cancer the spring before her fiftieth birthday, I was given a pristine white glassybaby simply named "Remembrance," along with instructions from my dear friend Arlys to light it anytime I found myself especially missing Kathy or longing to honor her memory. In this way, a simple piece of glass has bravely held out the light of gratitude and grace against the dark night of grief and loss.

I think we all ask the same question of ourselves, knowing that we are just one simple baby vessel for the light of Christ:

do we really have something of value to offer the world? It takes courage to trust that the light of Christ will make us luminous with warmth that draws many into his love. But as we submit to the fires of formation, and allow the breath of God to fill and shape us, that is exactly what he does.

Compelled by the beauty and simplicity of these translucent holders of light, I put pen to paper one day and created this little poem.

Luminous

First liquid
Furnace formed
Till solid, smooth, simple,
Unadorned
Hollowed, humble
Holding hues
Waiting to receive
Wax and wick (trust, belief)
Now luminous
Flame is lit
First the burning
Then the shedding light
Layers of translucent glass
Holding colors bright
Breath of art
Work of heart
Blaze into the night
Yes, fire-wild God, set the world ablaze through me.

soul souvenirs

1. When have you made a decision to follow a call during a crisis, and found that it lit up your life and offered warmth and peace to others?

2. What expressions of gratitude and grace have lit up a dark season in your life? How are you leaning into gratitude and grace right now?

chapter 21

magic and miracles

God always answers us in the deeps, never in the shallows of our soul. AMY CARMICHAEL

My blond-haired, slightly freckled, round-faced (enhanced by round-rimmed glasses), younger son, Jackson, is obsessed with magic. With a few props given to him in a magician's kit, he has perfected the art of several basic tricks to an impressive degree of showmanship. Last week, during one of his first free days of summer vacation, he took a TV tray, a few props, and a tin can labeled "donations" and stood outside our neighborhood Whole Foods grocery exclaiming to anyone within striking distance, "Come see a magic trick that will blow your mind!"

Living as we do in the heart of downtown Seattle, our grocery is stationed strategically near a busy bus stop, populated in great part by Amazon employees commuting from the multi-building campus dominating our neighborhood.

My husband and I lingered several feet away, close enough

to keep him safe, far enough away to blend into the crowd. We were prepared to recruit customers on the sly if he lingered sadly alone (and provide some small change for them to drop into his repurposed soup can). However, to his delight and our great surprise, he entertained a host of bored and waiting commuters and earned eighteen dollars in donations in just under half an hour. Now that's magic to a boy! Of course, what Jackson could never have comprehended was that the "magic" taking place was that a group of weary workers were being transported momentarily from their individual worries and complex realities back into the wonder years of childhood innocence and enthusiasm. And it was this "magic" that stirred their hearts and roused their generosity.

Yesterday I was thinking about the kind of magic shows we long for as adults when I took a walk with my friend Lori, mother of six (five boys and one girl). Her daily life holds a complexity of drop-offs and pick-ups and show-ups (for ballgames, band concerts, school plays, youth group activities) that takes my breath away. Somehow, in this mix, she added an extended assignment as a substitute teacher that lasted for several weeks toward the end of the school year.

In our conversation, Lori conveyed to me the utter exhaustion she felt one day in dealing with her out-of-control class (the same one that had so depleted the regular teacher, she was down with a critical case of mono). That day Lori had just five free minutes to sneak out for a quick coffee at a nearby stand. When she arrived, desperately needing the magic of a little caffeine pick-me-up, she discovered the barista had disappeared, leaving a sign that simply said, "Back soon." Lori stood there as long as she could, watching her precious break tick away until her dreams of an infusion of energy were just clouds in her imaginary coffee. Then, just in the nick of time, the barista returned and apologetically served her a complimentary coffee.

As Lori watched her work, she spotted a discreet tattoo on the barista's wrist, four small words: "Be still and know." Tears rimmed her eyes as she recounted the miracle moment, God's presence made visible to her by the emblazoned wrist of an unknown barista. Lori completed the tattooed thought out loud, "That I am God." And they stood there together, two harried women experiencing a shared miracle ("wherever two or more have gathered in my name, there I am, also"), and that little walk-up coffee hut had become holy, "the kingdom of God is among us."

This conversation about the difference between magical thinking and authentic miracles and how mixed up our longings can be was made all the more precious by Lori's own Jesus journey. Following the birth of her sixth child, and fifth boy (whom she adores), Lori faced a crisis of faith. She had prayed genuinely for a girl, longing for her daughter to have the miracle of a sister. So sincere was her prayer, so powerful was her belief in God's promise to honor the desires of her heart, that in faith she hadn't had an ultrasound and had chosen only a darling baby girl "coming home" outfit to take to the hospital. When a baby boy was born, adorable though he was, something in her faith dried up that day, triggering a painful season of spiritual anguish, a sort of "dark night of the soul" that stretched out before her for several months. There had been a miracle of birth, but there had not been the magic of a girl, and she had been looking for magic.

Now most of us would have a "dark night of the soul" simply from the exhaustion of a sixth (and surprise) pregnancy while parenting five other little ones already. At the time, Lori was a member of a small group which I had recently formed as a result of feeling God's clear call to do so (a group which has sustained me for more than a decade and is still going strong). Candid with her doubts, her disappointments in God, and the depression she was wading through, Lori opted out of our group's shared prayer times for a season. But she always stayed invested in the circle of friends, loving and being loved, allowing us to believe and pray and hope and share her journey with her. Even while we didn't fully understand the complexity of her reaction to that unanswered prayer for a girl, as her friends we easily extended to her a deep grace in this mysterious crisis.

Looking back, Lori says it was in the context of our group of friends that the eyes of her heart began to see things differently. In fact, Lori recently dreamed of a broken contact lens that couldn't be repaired; it just needed to be replaced. Lori can recall a conversation woven throughout the fabric of our group's interactions during her dark season about the difference between seeing God's promises through the lens of a magical faith versus the profound belief in the miraculous purposes of God no matter the momentary view. A traveling saint who is one of my heroes of faith, Amy Carmichael, herself a pioneering missionary to India, faced the mystery of unanswered prayers after an accident left her bedridden for decades. During that time she wrote these words: "But God always answers us in the deeps, never in the shallows of our soul."[5]

Somewhere over those days and months Lori replaced those old broken contacts with a new set of eternal ones. She had moved from the shallows of her soul to the deeps. Now she wading in miracles of God's presence all around her, every day and everywhere, even on the tattooed wrist of a tardy barista!

soul souvenirs

1. In what ways do you relate to the longing for God to work magic in your life? How do you tend to cope with your disappointment when he doesn't?

2. Have you had the experience of God working a miracle that answered an even deeper need than the one you were preoccupied with? How did it change you?

5. Amy Carmichael, *Candles in the Dark* (Fort Washington, Pa.: Christian Literature Crusade, 1982), 86.

chapter 22

shorebreak

✣ *Trust is a golden pathway to heaven.*

SARAH YOUNG

Yesterday, alongside my boys, husband, and dear family friends, I shared a joyful experience of playing in waves crashing on the beach. The waves were unusually large, the biggest seen around this Maui beach in twenty years. Surfers had been gathering from the corners of the earth at the world-famous surfing beach known as "Jaws" for chances to ride forty-to-fifty footers. It was epic. On our side of the island, the waves hovered in the five-to-ten-foot range, but don't let those smaller numbers fool you; they loomed large. All of this was sheer joy for our group of five boys, ages eleven to seventeen, on their way to manhood. Wrangling waves is one of those rites of passage that urges them forward. However, being a card-carrying member of the worried moms' club, I was rather preoccupied with the sign we had all trotted by minutes earlier: "Warning! Dangerous shorebreak. Serious injury could occur. When in doubt, don't go out."

It took me the longest of anyone in our party to get beyond

135

the crashing "shorebreak" of the shallows to the relative safety of those glorious rising waves in the deeper sea, farther from shore. Of course, any sea lover knows it's that in-between place, not close enough to shore to be protected, not far enough into the deeps to be safe, where the most danger lies. Where there are shorebreak conditions, the waves don't come rolling in but barrel down with a force that reminds you of your place within the laws of nature and the providence of God.

Once out into the deeper waters, it was thrilling. I was quickly overcome by the beauty of the sky and water, dancing waves pulling me into their musical movements. Then it happened. A swell that came too high and too fast for me to get ahead of. I found myself at exactly the wrong place at the right time. A wall of water cascaded down on me, pulling me under, grounding me face first into the ocean floor. I struggled; I tumbled over and around; I felt my chest pounding and couldn't find air. I fought so hard against the wave that the muscles in both of my calves contracted and my legs spasmed. Salt and sand were everywhere, great gulps of it down my throat, in my eyes. When I emerged from the water in the aftermath, my husband said that the look on my face was sheer terror. As if I expected to find apocalyptic devastation and no survivors. Later, as my liquid puddle of nerves solidified into a solid sense of self, I began to notice just how much sand I had acquired in my sea spin, an impressive collection housed inside my suit.

That experience was so intensely physical, but its spiritual reality was not lost on me. As a spiritual quester, I love walking along the beach of my faith. The beauty of those deeper waters is magnificently stirring—from a distance. I feel inspired and delighted by them, and collect treasures along the shore in the form of verses and sermons and moments of true growth. I want to build a cozy beach house on the shore and always be close to it.

Then comes the invitation to enter the water. Wade in and join the dance. Risk forgiveness; live generously; lay down my preferences; abandon my need for approval; choose the course of obedience. But the thing is, I can't get to those deeper, dancing waters without making my way through the shorebreak zone. And warning! It's dangerous there. Swells come too fast and too high. Crises arise to pummel my soul and upend my dreams and shatter my joy. Forgiveness has a cost; dying to self is a daily struggle; even my very capacity to abandon my own preferences in obedience sometimes plants me face down in the sand. This journey isn't about staying here, in the shorebreak zone, but about moving beyond it to the dancing waters of trust. But I have to move through this place to get beyond. And this place is a crisis of faith.

One of my quirky preferences is being home, in my city of Seattle, with my closest circle of family and friends. I don't crave adventure; what I crave is connection. I am a loyal soul. My ideal life is one of deep ministry hidden away in a university or church community. This is the journey I embarked on with my husband Les nearly thirty years ago. When it became clear that writing was a part of that calling for us, I was delighted. Writing is a hidden, solitary discipline, practically monastic. I wanted to love people in small circles. Student discipleship groups, mentoring connections, classrooms populated with a modest collection of learners, our local body of Christ.

What I never anticipated and would never have chosen is the very transient life of speaking and traveling that began to unfold for us. As we began to write about marriage, simply in response to the needs of the students surrounding us, we began to receive invitations to come and share with others. Those invitations snowballed, and soon we were speaking in different cities about forty weeks a year. Not my preference, to say the least. I fasted. I prayed. I negotiated with God. My inner resistance was so overwhelming that from time to time when an event would cancel for one reason or another, Les would say to me with a knowing grin, "You prayed against this one, didn't you?" But in unmistakable ways God always said to me, "Leslie, this is my way for you; walk in it."

After our first child was born, a fragile one-pound preemie, a season of intensive care and surgeries and hospitalizations followed. God had grounded me as caregiver to this precious life. But then came an unexpected call from the governor of Oklahoma. And this time, we were uprooted for an entire year, medically fragile toddler and all, to serve as "marriage ambassadors" for a state doing an amazing work to reverse a desperately high divorce rate. Shorebreak! I tumbled around, terrified, upended. For me it was a crisis of trust. Of not knowing if this obedience would put my fragile toddler (with a cluster of problems gathered into the diagnosis "failure to thrive") in serious jeopardy. Never mind rending my own loyal soul from its Seattle soil and the cozy cottage of faith set farther back on the safer shores of obedience.

I love a short spiritual classic entitled *Abandonment to Divine Providence*, a simple collection of letters written by French Jesuit priest Jean-Pierre de Cassade to a group of nuns under his spiritual direction in the 1700s. In these letters he describes two levels of trusting obedience: active and passive.

Active loyalty means obeying God by fulfilling the duties of our lives; passive loyalty means that we lovingly accept all that God sends us each moment of the day, abandoning our own agendas and trusting that our happiness and holiness can be found in the unfolding "Divine Providence" of our lives. De Cassade instructs that every time we feel in our hearts a desire or a fear, or have ideas and form projects regarding our own interests or those of our family and friends, we simply say to God, "Lord, I sacrifice this all ... may all that you please, all that you wish, happen ... give me the right thought at the right time, thus I shall do nothing but follow what you inspire, and accept in advance either good or adverse results." He then goes on to give the nuns this little gem of guidance: "Let your fears and desires drop like a stone into the sea."

Proverbs puts it this way:

> *Trust GOD from the bottom of your heart;*
> *don't try to figure out everything on*
> *your own.*
> *Listen for GOD's voice in everything you*
> *do, everywhere you go;*
> *he's the one who will keep you on track.*
> *Don't assume that you know it all.*
> *Run to GOD! Run from evil!*

Your body will glow with health,
    your very bones will vibrate with life!
Honor GOD with everything you own;
    give him the first and the best.
    (Proverbs 3:5 – 7)

I don't know what fear or desire stones you hold in your hand that need to be dropped into the sea. I know that at any given time I have a handful in mine. I know only that even in the shorebreak, when the waters pummel and twist, God can be trusted. And that the deeper dancing waters of the surrendered life, that actively loyal trust, are calling. And that what awaits us there in "Divine Providence" is a story not bound by our fears or desires — and is therefore beyond compare.

soul souvenirs

1. What fear or desire stones are you holding right now? What, if anything, is keeping you from dropping them into the sea?

2. Where do you find yourself right now on the Jesus journey? Are you in a cozy seaside cottage just being inspired by the beauty of your faith, in the shorebreak getting pummeled, or in the deeper waters of trust enjoying the dance? What do you need most from God in this place?

growth spurts

Under The Mercy every hurt is a fossil link in the great chain of becoming.   Eugene Peterson

Last week my eleven-year-old son, Jackson, lost three teeth in one day, two at school and one later that same evening at home. This happened on the heels of another two-tooth weekend, and preceded the loss of still one more tooth the very next week. Jackson is my "foodie" who relishes eating, and this has definitely put a crimp in his style. To add insult to injury, he is in a major growth spurt resulting in his lower jaw (which grows the same way feet and arms and legs do) outpacing the growth of his upper jaw. Because of this, his jaw pops annoyingly with each and every bite. The dentist says it's all perfectly temporary and just part and parcel of the unwieldy process of growth. His awkward appearance has given those of us who love him loads of laughter, which he endures good-naturedly, along with gaping grin, too-tight shoes, and barely passable-in-length Levi's.

But his growth spurt has also been something of a living parable for me. Most of the time growth happens slowly, imperceptibly, and in hiddenness. And then there are the fully-to-be-expected moments of normal change (the odd loose tooth that wiggles free, the clumsiness that follows disproportionally super-sized feet, the eruption of an unwanted blemish, the squeak of a changing voice). These markers of growth are notable, and even if they are not altogether pleasant, are often marked by little rites of initiation or celebration.

But then, often out of the blue, come the days that catch us off guard, knock the wind out of us, or a handful of teeth. The first loss is taken in stride. The second one gets our attention. But the third one. It sends us over the edge of ordinary and into the abyss of crisis. It spins us into a time of pain and darkness and bewilderment. It turns out that our smile was resting heavily on the scaffolding of baby teeth, which have abandoned us, leaving us with a fairly useless mouth full of gaping holes. It's hard to sink our teeth into the promises of God's goodness and provision when all we have are gums. And if the professionals tell us this is growth, it's hard to believe them, because what it feels like is something else altogether.

When Mother Teresa's personal journals and private letters to her spiritual advisor were made public a few years ago, they revealed an intense interior darkness that stunned the world. Not just a few bad days, or a season of extraordinary doubt, but five decades shaped largely by overwhelming anguish, dryness, and discouragement. After years of intimate connection with her Savior there came a feeling of creeping separateness from God, of abandonment by her Savior, of emptiness and darkness that stretched on and on and on.

What added to her anguish was the fear that her inner

losses were turning her obedience to Christ into a parody. That she was not only unlovable, but that her very life of service to the poorest of the poor would further dishonor her Father because even if it was done in his name, it was not accompanied by a deep personal assurance of his presence. In this way, the Nobel Peace Prize–winning icon of joy and peace and service suffered privately and intensely. Reading these journals and her letters, which have been collected into a book entitled *Come Be My Light*, was one of the scariest things I've ever done.

In a way, I came to a new place of understanding for the disciples in the garden that terrible suffering night before the soldiers came for Jesus. Here, his dearest friends were rendered incapable of being fully present, of remaining prayerful and wide awake in the moment when it mattered most. I wonder to myself if the suffering and struggle of Jesus was just too much for them to bear. Blood streaming down anguished cheeks; repeated pleading that God would not ask this huge and horrific thing of him. The utter devastation that God his loving Father could will such a thing, that someone who loved him could, simultaneously, require it of him and abandon him. The scandalous surrender of a Son to his Father, in nevertheless-not-my-will-but-yours-be-done obedience. It's too much to bear. It triggers my fight-or-flight instincts, and if sleep is my only way to fly away, then I will go to sleep. Escape this crisis of faith before it unravels us both.

Last year my mom had a terrible accident, crushing her wrist, arm, and shoulder. Her bones were protruding through the skin and her injuries were severe. In the ER, I stood beside her stretcher and held her while she cried anguished cries and squeezed me tight, pushing against the pain. I wanted to be fully present with all my heart, but my love for her mingled with my awareness of the seriousness of her injuries. Finally the intensity of her pain overwhelmed me with anxiety until, mid-prayer, I quietly melted into a puddle of unconsciousness, fainting to the floor.

Sometimes life forms itself into inexplicable crisis, devastating not only the person herself, but everyone who loves her. My friend Lucy lost her little boy on Christmas day when he drowned in the neighbor's pool. It is a universal truth that the loss of a child is life's darkest day. She somehow found the faith to carry on with grace. Then, many years later, her robust husband Dennis was taken in the prime of his brilliant career with a brain tumor, leaving Lucy once again to carry on bravely, alone. How we celebrated when God's restorative grace came in the form of Wayne, an old faithful friend and a newly passionate love. But cancer came like an uninvited guest to their wedding, sitting on Wayne's side of the aisle. And all of us who love Lucy have tried to stay in the garden with her, wide awake while she prays through. But I have to confess, it's tempting to doze off, to allow distractions to provide an escape. Sometimes it hurts too much to stay fully present and aware. We want to be able to fix things, or at the very least to erase the pain; and when we can't, the anxiety can be overwhelming.

Jesus found strength in his single loneliest moment of obedience, at the peak of his suffering, in the crisis of his abandonment, through the poetic prayers of King David. Recorded in his own spiritual journal and known to us as Psalm 22, it was

David's prayer that Jesus uttered and embodied to its utmost, "My God, my God, why have you forsaken me?" These were the words that led him to the finish line, and carried him home.

Mother Teresa, the little nun of Calcutta, was greatly helped by a spiritual advisor who entered into her pain and gave her a new frame for it. He assured her that there was nothing she had done to cause her pain and nothing within her human power to cure it, and therefore there was no place whatsoever for guilt because of it. Furthermore, he reminded her that feeling the presence of Jesus is not the only evidence of his presence with us; that the very longing for God was itself a gift from God and a sign of his presence within her. And finally he assured her that her feeling of God's absence was the spiritual side of the beautiful work she was doing for Jesus; that those she served had also felt abandoned and utterly alone, and she was participating in the fellowship of their sufferings in her own soul. These words of counsel held her heart as the psalm of David had held the heart of Jesus, causing her to finally say, "I have come to love the darkness."

In my own journal, inspired by the recent parable of my son's lost trinity of teeth, this poem emerged.

Baby Teeth

My mind reviews my
Losses
Like my son's tongue
Seeks out his recent
Missing tooth.

In a way
This whole life is a mouth full
Of baby teeth.
The permanent ones
Will sprout someday
In our gaping gums
And we'll sink those teeth
Into Eternity
And smile.

I can't begin to answer the big questions that loom larger than life when we rub shoulders with darkness. Days when our heavenly Father leaves us seemingly deserted and vulnerable, or asks for the impossible step of obedience without so much as a hint of solace. Days when we feel ourselves to be not only friend forsaken but utterly God forsaken as well. But I do believe with all my heart in the resurrection (and the accompanying and ultimate joy). No matter how dark the now, there will be the joy before us then; and the promise of this is what allows me to know at the core of my being that God is powerful enough to transform evil into good even if I don't see it this side of eternity. That's why tears of longing mingled with joy stung my eyes when my friend Clare signed off on a recent email, "Longing for heaven." Some fine day there will be no more baby teeth to lose, just permanent pearly whites and an ear-to-ear smile. Amen.

soul souvenirs

1. When have you had to be brave enough to share in a painful season with someone you love? What did you learn from that experience?

2. Have you ever felt abandoned by almost everyone—family, friends, and God? How did you respond?

chapter 24

bright abyss

To see a candle's light one must take it into a dark place.   UrsULA Le Guin

One of my favorite places on earth is Cannon Beach, Oregon, a hamlet nestled west of Portland along the Pacific Northwest coast. Surrounded by a symphony of natural beauty—including forests, rivers, and the Oregon Coast Range—this little stretch of beach is home to Haystack Rock, one of the largest rock formations found along the coast and a treasure trove for tide pool enthusiasts (of which I am one). When I recently learned that Cannon Beach was named one of *National Geographic* magazine's "World's 100 Most Beautiful Places," I had two simultaneous thoughts: "Of course!" and "Oh no!"

This is one of those towns whose charm lies as much in the feeling that not only is it beyond glorious but beyond the awareness of a great many people. Thus, a sort of local, private pleasure. And as if to underscore that fact, the coffee roaster that functions as community center for Cannon Beach is called the Sleepy Monk. Aptly named. This is a place that inspires deep reflective moods and slows your soul to an otherworldly pace. A place to hide. A place to seek.

To this backdrop of aesthetics, add nostalgia. For my husband Les, whose family had a little beach shanty along this stretch of coast, where he and his brothers shared childhood misadventures; and for us as a honeymooning couple, writing the first pages of our own story on these ocean shores. And so it is no surprise that during one of the darkest seasons of my husband's life, the decline and death of his father, he woke up one morning with a sudden and irrepressible urge to go to Cannon Beach.

Within a few hours our family was on the road, headed to this healing hideaway. The drain of it all—the dearness of Les's love for this great man and the dread of his loss— had deteriorated Les's immune system: he had been fighting a low-grade sinus infection for what seemed like an eternity. Sadness had wrapped a blanket around him, and the rest of us had crawled beneath it too. Scientists tell us that emotions are measurably contagious. Our brains have been wired with what are called "mirror neurons" that brilliantly receive and reflect the undercurrents of feelings in those who surround us. In fact, this capacity is so powerful that emotions can be measurably transmitted three persons removed from their original source (the happiness or sadness of a friend of a friend of a friend can literally shape my mood). In a way, nothing we feel is ever truly private. Of course, the recipient of the message always makes a choice in his or her response—some choose empathy and others apathy. But there is always the choice.

When someone we love has fallen into a dark mood, it

can be downright scary. The act of "entering in" feels almost life threatening and even, for some of us, a bit panic inducing. I stood peering down into my husband's soul, and what I saw there was a hole so great and deep that I could not measure it against anything I had known of him before. It was an apparent abyss of grief.

Our family bravely ventured on toward the coast, sailing in our car along the freeway, away from all the sadness toward this bright place of memory and monumental beauty. We arrived in the early evening, just in time to walk along the beach by the light of the setting sun. The wind blew and the fires sparkled and the salty air filled our lungs. We exhaled.

At dinner there was an incident. Gathered around a table at a tiny Italian cafe, I had attempted to share the first bite of my entree with Les, and instead turned my full plate of food upside down to crash loudly on the terracotta-tiled floor. It was jarring and halted conversation around every table in the entire cafe.

Weary from our spontaneous travels, beach walk, and unrelaxing dinner, we went to check into the little inn near the beach, only to discover there were no vacancies. This ritual was repeated until every single hotel in this seaside town had been tried and tested. There simply were no rooms available. Finally, around midnight, Les remembered a nearby Christian conference center where we had been invited to speak a number of times over the years; perhaps they would have mercy on us and give us a place to spend the night. After a negotiation that resulted in our entire family registering for a conference we were obviously not able to attend, we bedded down in a room of bunk beds. We were thankful, but not comfortable (since we hadn't packed towels and soap or blankets).

The psychologist Carl Jung coined the term *synchronicity*, which he used to describe what he thought of as meaningful coincidences that happen in our lives. Such as those times when we've been preoccupied with thoughts of someone, and right that moment they call. Or those seasons of life when our inner world has a certain mood that our outer world seems to organize itself around (Les feeling lost and a bit homeless with his dad slipping away, my plate slipping out of my hands and crashing, finding no hotel for the night). Sometimes, when we are in a dark place, it feels as if the whole world is out to get us.

Being in the dark is scary and lonely, and it is easy to get lost. And when the darkness goes on and on, it can begin to feel like a space so big it cannot be measured: an abyss. The single best thing about being in the darkest of dark places is how powerful one tiny flame can be. Light a candle in the darkness, and suddenly what seemed infinite is shown to be finite. One kind word, one feeble attempt at humor, one gentle touch from a soul friend. By some miracle of God's goodness, we are able to push into the bleakest moments with the simplest of love's signs.

At our church we have a tradition of giving prayer quilts to people whose lives have grown cold and dark. The quilt, lovingly sewn by members of the church, is draped over a stand beside the altar while the entire church prays for them. Those who feel led kneel individually at the quilt and tie a knot in the purposely unfinished threads while they pray. In this way all the prayers of the people are tied up in warmth and delivered in love. The quilt doesn't cure the disease or reverse the loss or solve the problem. But, like the light flickering in a dark place, it warms the soul and somehow changes everything.

A number of years ago Judith Viorst wrote a children's book that so resonated with people (parents and children alike) that it quickly became a bestseller. Written for her son, Alexander, and she simply titled it, *Alexander's Terrible Horrible Awful No Good Very Bad Day*. Sometimes just being willing to enter into a terrible day and to name the hard things unfolding in it is all it takes to contain the damage to the soul of the one having it. Our ability to validate and name the experience of someone who is walking through overwhelming suffering is powerful. Paradoxical. Though it feels like underscoring the bad thing will make it even worse, psychologists—who make a living doing the simple and profound work of really listening, truly seeing, with accurate understanding—know it does quite the opposite.

Abraham (still Abram at the time) and Sarah (still Sarai) got tired and desperate while waiting for the fulfillment of God's promise to make Abraham the father of a great nation, and so they involved Hagar in their earthly scheme to accomplish God's plan. Hagar was Sarah's Egyptian servant, and at Sarah's prompting she became a sort of surrogate to Sarah's infertility and bore Abraham a son, Ishmael. What unfolded in the aftermath of this conception is a story of conflict and emotional undercurrents that every woman alive can relate to. Jealousy, feelings of competition, hurt, and anger. We know Sarah was extraordinarily beautiful (remember the soap opera Abraham had created in Egypt when he asked her to pretend to be his sister so her beauty would not be his death penalty).

But we all know how infertility can suck the very marrow from our bones, and Sarah must have felt more brittle, hollow, and aching than words can tell to resort to a this many-shades-of-gray solution.

Finally things got so heated between them that pregnant Hagar ran away into the desert wilderness. Lost and alone, vulnerable and afraid, Hagar had entered the abyss. She wasn't exactly innocent, and yet she wasn't all to blame. And mostly that is our story too. Life is complicated, and so are the people we love. It's not that our motives are purely right or entirely wrong. Barrenness leads to brokenness. Brokenness leads us down paths of desperation. Desperate people do desperate things, and consequences spin beyond our control. Hagar had never felt more invisible and powerless. And it was here that an angel of God found her beside a desert spring and gave her wisdom and understanding about her future, although it would not be without suffering. For this lost woman, being found by God in the wilderness was so powerful it literally changed everything. She named that place "God-Alive-Sees-Me Spring," praying the deepest, awe-filled, faith-igniting prayer, "You're the God who sees me!" Being seen in our wilderness, known in our suffering, validated in our pain, is transformational.

One of the wilderness moments for me of late has been the journey of menopause. Extra weight has collected itself around my waist against all efforts to the contrary. My moods are inexplicably darker and stormier, and all senses of girlish beauty have distanced themselves from me. Caught in this hormonal vortex, I can feel as if my feminine value is swirling down the drain. It's a feeling that gives me newfound empathy for Sarah. Against this backdrop my husband quite innocently and good-naturedly (and without any thought of comparison or disparagement) complimented the evident beauty of one and then another of my girlfriends. And he is right, they are both lovely, and I want to relish that beauty — female masterpieces of God's artistic glory. But my own sense of dwindling loveliness had depleted my generosity of spirit, and the compliments to others felt like insults to me. Aided by supercharged hormones, the floodgates opened and the tears came until I marveled there could possibly be even one more. I pulled myself together and went through the motions of my busy life, but the undercurrent wasn't one of gratitude or joy.

Later that day as I was sitting at my desk, I happened to glance at the ribbon board above it. Tucked into those intersecting ribbons are all the scraps of memory and bits of anticipation that make up the mosaic of my current life. The details for the church high school retreat John will go to next week, the dog groomer's contact information, even a postcard from Cannon Beach. But in this moment, my eyes fell on a little folded piece of white typing paper that my husband had given me as a homemade card a few months ago on our anniversary. It featured a photo of me, standing in front of one of Seattle's quirkiest places — the gum wall.

Located in Post Alleyway, hidden away beneath one of the city's most popular spots — Pike Place Market — this narrow brick-wall-lined alcove is covered from the ground up with globs of colorful chewing gum that stretch as far as the eye can see. It is bright and strange and interesting and repulsive all at the same time. In this moment here I was, hair drawn back into a ponytail, leaning forward with my tongue extended, creating the optical allusion that I am actually licking the wall. Yuck! The caption Les added to the moment was simply, "That's my girl."

Something about that completely unscripted, decidedly unglamorous image reminded me that the people I love don't ✗ need me to perform or to be perfect. All they ask of me is simply to be in the moment, fully present, heart wide open. When I take on life with that commitment, even gum-wall goofiness becomes—well, maybe not beautiful—but somehow precious to share.

And the truth is, often the deeper the pain and the darker the abyss, the more powerful the single, small, simple act of hearing, seeing, sharing, and caring can be. Any reminder that we are seen, known, heard, desired, and loved pushes back the night. Soul friends: squeeze the hand, linger over the story, hold open the door, offer the prayer, ask the follow-up question, shoot off the text, make eye contact, and give away your warmest smile. Listen to the undercurrent of emotions in those around you, and when they are dark, don't be afraid. Entering into the darkness will not consume you nor will it push them farther in. Psychologists have a shorthand way of conveying all of this: "Name it to tame it; connect and redirect." It's just another way of saying that when someone is flooded with dark emotions such as sadness, fear, anger, or despair, there is true therapy in seeing, touching, and encouraging. Take what is dark and make it light; take an abyss and make it bright ... even a loss as significant as a beloved parent or as tender as fading youth.

soul souvenirs

1. When have you felt invisible only to have an encounter that reveals you are seen by God?

2. Who or what is being a light to you in the darkest places of your life right now? How?

chapter 25

angel food cake

*Above all, I think that the willingness and the cour-
age to keep on trying develops best if there is someone
we love close by who can lend us some of the strength
we do not yet have within ourselves.*   FRED ROGERS

Elijah is my favorite Old Testament prophet. Not just for all
the obvious reasons, like being a spiritual giant whose prayers
changed the weather and who understood that God was ready
to make himself known in a cosmic fireworks battle against
Queen Jezebel and her false god, Baal. And not because he was
a man who walked with God so closely that he was escorted
to heaven in a chariot of fire. No, Elijah is my favorite prophet
because mingled together with moments of monumental spiritual strength are equally stunning moments of utter frailty
and personal weakness.

   On the same day, Elijah had called down both fire and
rain from heaven, demonstrating God's might and ending
the spiritual and physical drought in Israel. Afterward, supercharged by God, he outran King Ahab's chariot on an ultra-
marathon of escape from the wicked — and now humiliated

157

and enraged—king and queen. Once far away and safe, Elijah collapsed in the shade of a broom bush, and the Bible tells us that this man of great faith who had prayed for rain to stop and then again, three years later, for rain to resume, prayed for God to take his life. *The Message* says it this way: "Enough of this, GOD! Take my life—I'm ready to join my ancestors in the grave!" (1 Kings 19:4). Elijah was obviously having a profound crisis of faith—and he simply gave up and fell sound asleep. The children's "Now I lay me down to sleep ... if I should die before I wake" prayer sums it up. Knowing God's track record, I am sure Elijah fully expected that God "his soul would take."

Instead, Elijah's sleep was so sound that an angel had to shake him to wake him up. And Elijah found beside him a cake, right there in the middle of nowhere, that had been baked over a bed of coals (a warm and life-giving fire Elijah had not built), along with a jar of water, provisions he unquestioningly consumed. After a nap, a second nudge, and yet another helping of "angel food cake," Elijah was strengthened. The angel told him, "You've got a long journey ahead of you." Nourished by that heaven-sent meal, Elijah took off on a forty-day walk to the mountain of God, where, upon arrival, he crawled into a cave and promptly went back to sleep again.

It was here that Elijah had his heart-to-heart with the God of Angel Armies who had so recently dispatched a willing angelic foot soldier to strengthen him along his lonely way. And in that revealing conversation, God chose to show himself not in the shattering wind or in the raging fire or even in the tremoring earth, but in the gentleness of a quiet whisper—an act of pure grace, empathic beauty, and brilliant therapeutic alignment with Elijah's desperately low mood.

Elijah told God honestly, "I've been working my heart out, and I'm exhausted." And God's response to Elijah's crisis was the gift of a new companion, Elisha — coworker and future successor. Help for now, hope for later. A soul friend. A little foretaste of the heaven he was so ready to make his home.

Every one of us goes through moments of crisis when we need a helping of angel food cake to gain the strength to take another step on the journey. We've worked our heart out — in our marriage, with our teenager, on our job. Yet our best intentions have failed. We've prayed and served and given and cared, but it looks as if it's all been for naught. We hardly even care anymore; we can't find the strength to go on, so we just go to sleep — whether figuratively or literally.

One of the ways we go to sleep is to seek an escape. I have a dear friend whose faith and candor remind me much of Elijah. Occasionally she calls me when she feels exceptionally low and says, "Pray for me, Leslie; I'm thinking about my fantasy family again." And I know exactly what she means. So do you. Your escape might be another triple chocolate cupcake or a romance novel or a shopping spree. It might be Facebook or Pinterest or another glass of wine. It might even be something that looks virtuous on the surface, such as saying yes to another volunteer position that makes you feel important in a way those complicated relationships at home don't. It can be anything at all that moves you far away from that feeling of failure and fatigue and fruitlessness.

I love the story of Elijah because it shows me that God is okay with my frailty. He understands my limitations; he knows that when I've been working my heart out, I will become exhausted. He loves me enough to find me in the places where I have attempted to escape, and he will shake me back awake. This General of Angel Armies cares enough to dispatch angel food cakes to my wilderness hideaway, cakes that will sustain me for however long my journey ahead may be.

I was recently in one of those mid-journey slumps with my oldest son's health care. John, the one-and-a-half pound preemie, almost sixteen now, whose every breath of life is sheer miracle. After enduring the chaotic early years of nearly constant emergencies, endless neonatal intensive care stays, and multiple surgeries and therapies, John seemed at last to hit his stride around the first grade. But he still deals with complications, among them a quirky digestive system (he has yet to hit 100 pounds) and a too-small kidney that causes hypertension and resulting heart strain. These require daily medications and ongoing treatment and evaluation. Not a day goes by without my deep gratitude for his life, but even so, it has been a bit of a parental marathon run in the halls of children's hospitals, doctor's offices, and specialized clinics to keep pace.

And then I got behind. The nephrology (kidney) specialist had ordered a series of blood tests and X-rays for John, and I just hadn't had the wherewithal to follow through. There was summer vacation including summer camp, and then cross-country practice started before school had even resumed. Then there were meets every weekend and driver's ed (with after-school driving practice to schedule) and the new intensity of high school-level homework, not to mention the drama of an increasingly active social life (including girls)—and that doesn't even count my fifth grader's needs or my more-than-full-time professional commitments. Time had passed, day followed day, and before I knew it John was on the cusp of another birthday, with his yearly physical looming, when I realized with shame he had not yet had the important tests the doctor had ordered—ahem—six months prior. To add insult to injury, I was fully aware that it usually takes weeks of lead time to get an appointment booked. I was devastated for John and ashamed of myself, discouraged with my own foibles.

That's when it happened. A huge helping of angel food cake left by my weary side. One morning I faced down my inner demons, picked up the phone, and dialed Seattle Children's Hospital. Working with the schedulers in radiology, I started down the path of future appointment dates—with no results. Finally, after several futile minutes, the hospital employee on the other end of the line said to me, "Well, I have a cancellation at 4:00 p.m. today," to which I said, "Done!" Like icing on that angel food cake, we were able to schedule the blood work with absolute ease. Pulling up the orders that afternoon, the clerk looked at me quizzically and said, "I just want to make sure these are the correct ones; they are from quite some time ago." To which I smiled and said, "Yep, Mother of the Year award goes to me!" Within twenty-four hours of my tardy attempts, John's health care was up to date.

Of course, the journey before us is long. But in my moment of exhaustion, after working my heart out—yet still not measuring up—I was lent the strength of strangers and angels. It was as if God said to me that day, "Let there be cake—and by all means make it angel food."

soul souvenirs

1. When have you received a gift of sheer grace amidst your exhaustion that has refreshed you for the journey ahead?

2. When have you felt as if God gave you a season of rest or a partner to come alongside you in your limitations or tiredness? How is God doing this for you again right now?

part four
communion

When Jesus faced his final hours on earth, it was *love*
that was on his working agenda. "I've loved you the
way my Father has loved me. Make yourselves at home
in my love" (John 15:9). And, "This is my command:
Love one another the way I loved you ... Put your life
on the line for your friends" (John 15:12). And finally,
"I chose you, and put you in the world to bear fruit,
fruit that won't spoil. As fruit bearers, whatever you ask
the Father in relation to me, he gives you. But remember the root command: Love one another" (John
15:16–17). In the end, everything comes down to this:
a shared spiritual and emotional connection that tran-
scends the ordinary and ushers us into communion.
The Jesus journey is best traveled together—in the
sisterhood of traveling saints. It's not a solo adventure.
This expedition, sometimes tough and long, requires
soul friends.

chapter 26

jars of oil

I do not at all understand the mystery of grace—
only that it meets us where we are but does not leave
us where it found us. ANNE LAMOTT

Most days I start my morning with strong coffee and strong prayers. So I was amused recently to come across an ancient Ethiopian legend about the origins of coffee. Apparently more than a thousand years ago, a goatherd noticed that his goats became frisky and energetic after munching on certain berries, so he shared these magical berries with monks at a nearby monastery. Rejecting the goatherd's gift, the monks called the berries devilish and threw them into the fire. As the fire roasted the berries, a heavenly aroma filled the air. The monks then declared the berries divine!

I think about those frisky goats and those skeptical monks this morning, and thank God that coffee wasn't relegated to the Devil. Because my mornings with God are filled with the aroma of roasting beans, signaling to my physical being that it's time to tend to my spirit. This morning, while sipping my strong coffee, I turned to Psalm 5:1–3, a framework for strong prayers. "Listen, God! Please, pay attention! Can you make sense of these ramblings, my groans and cries? King-God, I need your help. Every morning you'll hear me at it again. Every morning I lay out the pieces of my life on your altar and watch for fire to descend."

I take great comfort in the company of the psalmist, who also finds that every morning there is fresh work to be done. Every day we need to place this ordinary life, this everyday sleeping-, eating-, going-to-work, and walking-around life, before God as an offering.

Lately I've been thinking about one of the parables Jesus told. A group of girlfriends (referred to as "virgins"), ten of them, are all waiting to join a wedding party. In those days, a typical wedding began when the groom went to the bride's home, where a ceremony would take place. Then, following the ceremony, the bride would go with the groom to his home, where an epic wedding party was thrown. The bridesmaids would take part in a little wedding parade, walking through the streets holding their torches, accompanying the bride and her groom to his home and the great wedding celebration.

In the story Jesus tells, the maids are watching and waiting for the groom. His coming is delayed beyond their expectations, and they all fall asleep. By the time that the shout comes announcing his arrival, it is night, and they all need to relight their lamps. The problem is, only half of them have oil to burn in the lamps (the wise girlfriends brought along jars of oil), while the other half have no oil (the silly girlfriends took lamps but no extra oil). The foolish girls ask the wise girls to share, but the wise refuse and tell the foolish to buy their own oil. So off go the unprepared girls to shop for oil. While they are away, they miss the parade, and everyone who was there to greet the groom has gone into the feast, locking the doors behind them. The foolish girls finally arrive much later and, hoping to join the festivities, they knock on the door, saying, "We're here; let us in." But to their surprise, the Master of the House says, "Do I know you? I don't think I know you!" And Jesus comments, "So stay alert. You have no idea when he might arrive."

As a child, whenever I heard this story, it always culminated in the Sunday school song, "Give me oil in my lamp, keep me burning, burning, burning … keep me burning till the break of day." And though I sang with gusto — wanting to be an insider at the party, and feeling a deep sense of urgency about being wise and prepared — I had absolutely no idea what else Jesus might want me to understand by telling this story.

Lately, however, I think I've come to understand those jars of oil the wise girlfriends held. I believe they were nothing more — and nothing less — than conversations logged with God, time spent knowing him and being transformed by him in the process. Without the jar filled with the oil of communion with God, the lamp of my heart has no power to light the darkness. But with the simple jar of a heart willing to embrace what the Spirit is doing in me — the very opposite of my childish, fear-based assumption that I needed to redouble my efforts to be perfect and prepared at all times — I have what I need to keep burning till the break of day. I love how Isaiah 66:2 describes the deep desire of God: "But there *is* something I'm looking for: a person simple and plain, reverently responsive to what I say."

I am all too aware that who I am and what I do is not an adequate match for even my ordinary days. One conversation with my sixteen-year-old can take me to my knees. I remember one morning on the thirty-minute drive to school John was frantically trying to complete the last bit of unfinished homework. As soon as his seat belt buckled, I started in, "encouraging" him to get right on it and not waste even one minute, as he had gone to bed last night promising to use this drive time wisely. Something in my tone set John off (imagine that in a teenager!), and he responded by slamming shut his notebook and saying, "I'm not going to do it; I don't care."

At that point, I matched his tone and raised him one, assuring him that he most certainly *would* be doing his homework, starting exactly right this minute! On the verge of tears, John angrily opened his book with an audible swishing sound and pulled out his assignment, which just happened to be for his Bible class. In a voice charged with anger, he read aloud his short essay assignment: *"Define peace."*

Ten seconds of total silence.

Then John, his younger brother Jackson, and I simultaneously dissolved into convulsive spasms of laughter. Tears streamed down my face, and our entire car was filled with shared joy. Talk about extra oil! Talk about entering into the gift of God's Spirit instead of redoubling my own efforts as a mom!

And so each morning, I'm at it again. I bring a full cup of strong coffee and my empty heart jar with me to be filled. I don't have a clue what events will unfold on any ordinary day. I rub shoulders with my family and friends, pack lunches, drive the kids to school, cook meals and do the dishes, show up at meetings, write and teach, take my mom to the doctor. But if I have spread out the pieces of my life on the altar, embracing God's Spirit within me, then my heart has been filled with the oil of responsive obedience no matter what emotions or challenges come my way. And the oil of prayer, of personal relationship and communion with God, lights up my life.

The book of Revelation talks about the great wedding supper of the Lamb (19:9). One thing I love is that the twenty-four elders of faith are pictured holding golden bowls full of incense, which are the prayers of the saints (5:8). Our prayers are not only a pleasing aroma to God; they are the light of our life — the jar of oil that will become the source of our flame.

soul souvenirs

1. How and when do you get your oil jar filled? In other words, when and how do you cultivate intimacy with God on a regular basis?

2. How does communing — or not communing — with God impact your ability to meet the challenges of your daily life?

north of expected

> *"I don't think the way you think. The way you work isn't the way I work. For as the sky soars high above earth, so the way I work surpasses the way you work, and the way I think is beyond the way you think."*
>
> ISAIAH 55:8

Not long ago, an ad campaign for Alaska Airlines splashed billboards all over Seattle with the simple words, "North of Expected." One of those billboards was prominently placed along my daily commute so that on some days I encountered it as often as four times. I should go on record saying that I feel a deep affinity for Alaska Airlines. Not only is it a Seattle thing, but its former CEO, Bruce Kennedy, became a dear friend when we served together on the executive committee of the board of CRISTA Ministries.

After retiring from Alaska Airlines, Bruce began investing his time in humanitarian work. Over the years, he and his wife Karleen have opened their home to shelter an ever-changing stream of refugees from all over the world. Many were the colorful stories he told of refugees acclimating to life in a culture so unlike the lands they had abandoned in the shadow of danger. Introducing them to things as simple as home appliances could be a highly complex (and decidedly comical) process. But Bruce's real enthusiasm was a company that manufactured planes designed to navigate dangerous and remote locations with heavy loads of cargo needed to aid missionaries around the world.

And yet it wasn't my deep respect for Bruce, or even a regional affinity for Alaska Airlines, that caused the billboard—a simply framed blue sky with a perfect puff of cloud and the phrase, "North of Expected"—to captivate me.

Recently I had been thinking hard about a conversation Jesus had with the Jewish leaders in the temple. Jesus had healed a lame man on the Sabbath, which had violently offended them. He admonished them: "You have your heads in your Bibles constantly because you think you'll find eternal life there. But you miss the forest for the trees. These Scriptures are all about *me*! And here I am, standing right before you, and you aren't willing to receive from me the life you say you want" (John 5:39–40).

These people believed in God and saw him as the true source of "eternal life." They took God's promises seriously, assured that he would deliver on his word to send them a Messiah who would restore the ruins of their lives. These were the faithful who lived the promise, "Oh, how could we ever sing God's song in this wasteland? If I ever forget you, Jerusalem, let my fingers wither and fall off like leaves. Let my tongue swell and turn black if I fail ... O dear Jerusalem, to honor you as my greatest" (Psalm 137:4–6). They put all their eggs in the God basket. He was their hope.

And then God, in his infinite wisdom, sent the very agent of healing and blessing they were longing for in a way that was so far "north of expected" that they could not discern his presence even when he was standing right before them. The Word made flesh, the Word no longer only on the printed page—but transferred to the flesh—life springing up in the wasteland. How could they miss it?

It's so tempting to come to the Bible as a textbook. God is the professor, "life" is the required course, and the syllabus announces that daily reading is a requirement for a good grade in the class. The goal, as a good "student," is to cover as much material as possible as quickly as possible, to master the concepts and apply them as answers on the comprehensive "exam" of my life.

Jesus seems to be suggesting that mastery of the Bible is not the goal. In fact, it seems that allowing the Word to master me, to form within me the capacity to see God at work in the world and to participate in it, is what the Bible is all about. He goes so far as to say, "I know that love, especially God's love, is not on your working agenda" (John 5:41).

Simeon was a man with his *heart* in the Bible, and love on his working agenda. The Bible describes him as "a good man, a man who lived in prayerful expectancy of help for Israel" (Luke 2:25). And when he encountered the infant Jesus in the temple, he immediately knew him as the Messiah. Taking the baby into his arms during his dedication ceremony, as Mary and Joseph stood speechless beside him, he said, "With my own eyes I've seen your salvation; it's now out in the open for everyone to see: A God-revealing light to the non-Jewish nations, and of glory for your people Israel" (v. 32). Not only that, but he saw deep into God's action in the world: "This child marks both the failure and the recovery of many in Israel. A figure misunderstood and contradicted ... But the rejection will force honesty, as God reveals who they really are" (vv. 34–35). The prophetess Anna was there, too, and with a seeing heart, "she showed up, broke into an anthem of praise to God, and talked about the child to all who were waiting expectantly for the freeing of Jerusalem" (v. 38).

Apparently, when love is on our working agendas, we come to the Bible with a spirit of humility, an inner posture of yieldedness, open to the mystery of God at work for purposes that reach far beyond our own agendas. In fact, the goal, paradoxically, is not the fulfillment of our expectations, but the relinquishment of them, to embrace God's agenda with *expectancy*.

This kind of seeing is more akin to the seeing of an artist. Most of us look at things and see them as we "expect" to. Past associations follow pathways in our brains to the fastest, simplest conclusions. An artist sees differently, abandons all of her preconceived expectations, and slows down, studying the image with expectancy, looking for the mystery and beauty that the object can reveal.

And then there are tricks of the trade, such as the "art squint." If you've ever tried to sketch something, you've probably found yourself squinting as you study your subject. The rods at the periphery of our eyes detect the nuances of light and dark, while the cones in the center give us color. When we need to see something with its contrasts highlighted, its shapes emphasized, we reflexively squint, using our lashes as a filter, separating with clarity the light from the dark, diminishing the gray.

I once took an art class in Florence, Italy. The class was held in the Basilica Santa Maria del Fiore, a cathedral crowned with the largest masonry dome in history—an enormous architectural feat of the Renaissance. The cathedral itself has been a center of reverent worship down through the centuries, as well as a setting for murder, intrigue, and politics both legitimate and corrupt. We were a small group of beginners learning about fresco, the unique art of mixing color pigment in lime water with fresh plaster to create enduringly permanent works of art. The urge to create art is nearly irrepressible when standing before great works like Michelangelo's "David," the seventeen-foot-high man-child with his sling. We were given guidance by our Italian instructor on how to create stencils with carbon, creating an approximation of a dot-to-dot to follow with paint and brush on the wet plaster.

The fresco artist must work quickly to stay ahead of the drying process. I was only beginning to understand that the great masters, such as Michelangelo, worked under the duress of speed, scale, and nearly impossible conditions. I remembered my undergraduate art appreciation course, taught by Professor Collins. He had wept as he stood reverently by the slides projected from his clunky overhead onto the classroom wall showing images of the ceiling of the Sistine Chapel. His stories had left a deep impression on me. How it was rumored that Michelangelo would go literally for weeks without stopping to so much as change his socks. His neglected, irritated skin peeled off with the fabric of his socks when he finally emerged from his work, leaving raw ankles and feet, painful and limping limbs.

Sitting comfortably at a table spread with supplies, lighted with afternoon sun and brushed with August breezes, I attempted valiantly to capture the field of sunflowers that had surprised me along the road on the island of Capri. This, for me, had been more cathedral than all the domes of Florence. My hands flew as I dipped and spread the brush. Gold, yellow, black, brown, green, and blue. The vision was so clear within me, and there it stayed! What emerged on my tile were mere patches of color, placeholders of memory. Even in Italy, sitting in the shadow of the Renaissance, inspired by the great masters, I was still not an artist.

When it comes to studying Scripture, the monastic tradition of *lectio divina* (a Latin phrase meaning literally "sacred reading") can serve as a pattern. St. Ambrose, St. Augustine, St. Benedict, these and a countless lineage of saints, have all engaged in this practice, taken this artistic posture, slowing down to ingest something as simple yet profound as a particular phrase or even a single word impressed upon them in prayerful reading. Meditating until the meanings find their way into the deepest places within. Encountering God in the text. Responding by allowing it to reveal to us the truth of who we really are. I love how the psalmist says it, "Silence is praise to you, Zion-dwelling God, and also obedience. You hear the prayer in it all" (Psalm 65:1–2).

Here is where art and Scripture converge. So many of us draw with abandon as children, delighted with the simple lines and circles that represent the people and objects we love, but so few of us draw as adults. Experts tell us that as our brain continues to develop, we achieve a stage of maturity, usually around twelve, that allows us to see clearly the utter disparity between what we have drawn and what we hope to represent. Once our eyes are opened to the gap between what we are attempting and what we are able to create, we give up in defeat. And that same kind of defeat often characterizes our faith. We throw up our hands and admit, "I am no saint!" But thanks be to God, we don't have to be.

In this posture, I am no longer the student reading my Bible as an assignment in life's syllabus, striving for a cosmic "A," attempting to master the text. Instead I am opening my heart to receive the words of God, allowing them to do the work God sent them to do, to complete their assignment within me, to fulfill his purposes of growth and fruit and nourishment for the hungry. I have become the fresco of God, allowing the Master to paint the colors that bring to life his inner vision of me. Jesus tells us, "But if you make yourselves at home with me *and my words are at home in you*, you can be sure that whatever you ask will be listened to and acted upon" (John 15:7, emphasis added).

Isaiah expressed it this way: "Just as rain and snow descend from the skies and don't go back until they've watered the earth, doing their work of making things grow and blossom, producing seed for farmers and food for the hungry, so will the words that come out of my mouth not come back empty-handed. They'll do the work I sent them to do, they'll complete the assignment I gave them" (Isaiah 55:10–11).

Now that is north of expected!

soul souvenirs

1. How have you been tempted to study the Bible to "master" it rather than allowing God to use it to "master" you? How did this impact your communion with God?

2. What are some of the things on your working agenda that might distract you from loving?

chapter 28

imperfect places

No need to perfect or perform. Just be a place for God — that is all.   ANGIE SMITH, *CHASING GOD*

My son Jackson has been practicing his experiment for the science fair at home. A dash of hydrogen peroxide, a pinch of dry yeast, a few teaspoons of water, and a squirt of dish soap combine to make an impressive eruption of dense but fluffy foam that comes rushing out of its container with a flourish. When it comes to science experiments, the greater the spectacle, the better the project (at least if you are a fifth-grade boy).

Today I was feeling like my life was a little too much like the spectacle of a science experiment — and as a fifty-year-old woman, that is *not* what I am going for. Like the ingredients in Jackson's project, mine were fairly commonplace — anxiety over a pressure-packed deadline, exhaustion from work and travel, complications from a snowstorm and an extra doctor appointment, and guilt over missing several special milestones in the lives of people I love. As I was rushing out the door to accomplish something small toward all of these ends, I discovered I had misplaced my keys. That is when the crazy eruption began.

Tears welled up and spilled over into sobs, mobilizing my husband to quickly join the search-and-rescue operation (search for the keys, rescue us both from this monumental meltdown that was creating a spectacular mess with our agendas). It took nearly an hour, and more than one tight hug of encouragement from my husband, and a host of arrow prayers, but I did finally find them hiding in a completely unlikely place.

As I hopped into the car, never more thankful for the sound of the door unlocking and the ignition engaging due to the priceless treasure of a key, I dialed (safely and legally on Blue Tooth) my prayer partner, hoping my lateness would not prevent the one thing I needed most right then—shared prayer. Grace, connection, prayer. And not just for me, but for a loved one in her life exhibiting science-experiment-like symptoms as well.

There are times in life when things just unravel. My friend Laurra discovered this in an epic way. For her son's tenth birthday she had hired a great Christian guy whose ministry was creating laser games for kids. To the delight of her son and all of his birthday guests, they had just successfully completed an undisputedly awesome laser gun contest in the woods behind their home, and Laurra was congratulating herself on a successful party. What mom can't relate to the utter relief and delight in that moment? She sent her husband out to pick up some pizzas for lunch while the boys played a little basketball. The high-energy portion of the party was over, and things were winding down to a fine finish.

At that exact moment, right after her husband drove off, one of her girlfriends hanging out during the party discovered her toddler had gone missing while she took a brief call on her cell. A quick thinker and aggressive problem solver, Laurra simply yelled, "Reward money to the first boy who finds this kid and brings him back safely to his mom!" This launched a serious search. The boys teamed up to scan the wooded yard while the grownups also began to search in earnest. Anxiety rose. Time was passing, and Laurra knew all too well that her wooded yard was rimmed by a dangerous ravine and a five-foot drop-off filled with water.

Just then, one of the boys came running to the house at full speed and slammed straight into the sliding glass door that he did not see or realize was closed. The door shattered, and shards of glass clung to every square inch of this boy like thorns from a prickly bush, covering him from head to toe. He began to ooze red in a multitude of places, like lava flowing beneath a volcanic crust. In God's infinite mercy, at that moment two other boys came running to the house, bringing the lost boy like a little lamb to the fold. They had discovered him trapped by a low tree branch just a few feet from the edge of the ravine where he could truly have drowned.

Quickly Laurra breathed a thank-you prayer to Jesus as she simultaneously turned her full attention to the stunned boy standing in her family room in the midst of a sea of shattered glass. Corralling the remaining boys into the garage to protect them from injury, she began to help him peel off his glass-covered layers of clothing to survey the injuries.

Precisely at this point Laurra's husband unwittingly pulled up with the pizza. Only fifteen minutes had passed, but it was as if the entire universe had shifted. Thankfully, the injured boy was truly fine, although he would spend a few hours in the ER enduring the delicate business of removing glass splinters. Who knew that a dash of boys, a pinch of wooded terrain, a teaspoon of unguarded time, and a few square yards of spotlessly transparent sliding glass could lead to such a spectacular eruption?

Sometimes our lives get messy even when we are giving our very best (like Laurra and her epic party), and we feel tempted to withdraw from the fray until we get our act together. Board up the sliding glass doors; fence off the woods; stop sending out the invitations. It's just too risky; someone (our image included) might get hurt. Thank goodness, that's not my gutsy friend Laurra. She has thrown away the need for perfection, the drive to perform, and extended an invitation to God to be present in every real moment that unfolds. Her welcome mat is out, and what you can count on is that the stories will be colorful, the laughter will be hearty, the humanity will put you at ease, and the invitation to join in is yours for the taking. The very next year when that birthday invitation arrived in the mail, I thought, *Are you kidding me? This is the hottest ticket in town, the most interesting party going. I wouldn't miss it for the world!*

Somewhere along the way I have discovered the counterintuitive truth that it is usually the less-than-perfect moments in our lives that connect us to people in the most amazing ways. Laurra's utter candor about the unraveling of her perfect party (and anything else that goes awry in her life) is one of her most winsome qualities.

One of the greatest privileges I've had has been to serve as a mentor for a few beautiful women who have been bold enough (or blind enough) to ask me to take on that role. Recently I was meeting with my adorable friend Brittany over lattes at the quintessential Seattle coffee shop Vivace. (The roaster and barista there are credited with the latte "art" culture, those amazing images created by pouring steamed milk over espresso in a flourish of artistic design.) It is always a high honor to be entrusted with this precious brand of friendship. Honestly though, I had to laugh about it, as Brittany seemed so nearly perfect to me already that I wondered what I had to offer her.

Our connection is deep for more reasons than just faith and kindred spirits. Like us, she and her husband Tim have committed themselves to live and minister in the heart of Seattle. Even as their family has expanded, adding first one, then two, and now three eye-catching ginger-haired girls to their family, they have resisted the trend to move out to the better schools and living spaces, and stayed put, raising their kids in this dense urban environment with a sense of mission that is not the least bit self-righteous.

And yet on this day Brittany's heart was heavy because one of her girls, a spirited toddler going through a persistent biting phase, had been acting out in a play group. Tears rimmed her eyes. As a young mom she was feeling not only weary and a little lost, but truly ashamed. She had so wanted to be the good example of motherhood and parenting with friends who were brand new to the faith and watching her every move for clues to this new life. Instead, on this occasion, her child was the *worst* offender.

My heart skipped a beat. Now I knew why I was here. With complete confidence and delight, I was able to tell her that her reaction to her daughter's humiliating biting phase was probably the single most inviting thing about her to those women at her church—her humanity as a mama. God would use this chink in her armor to become a hook that other women could hang their hat on and relate to. Since Brittany wasn't perfect, maybe they could find a way to believe they belonged on this Jesus journey too. I love how Paul puts it: "We can comfort those in any trouble with the comfort we ourselves receive from God" (2 Corinthians 1:4 NIV).

I used to believe that to step into my calling I needed to be polished, professional, and as perfect as humanly possible. When Les and I first began to receive calls to speak as a couple at marriage events and seminars across the country, I had extreme self-doubt and anxiety. I felt that the only credibility I could have as a teacher was if I were able to perfectly embody everything I taught. The fear was so crippling that I not only fasted and prayed—I found a therapist. It was immobilizing. I felt I had to mend every broken place in me (and therefore in my marriage) to qualify as a teacher. Only when I understood that our best teaching came from sharing our honest pilgrimage as a couple wholeheartedly committed to living into these ideals—*not* a couple under the pretense of having arrived at them—did God give me a genuine joy in using the gift of teaching he had given me.

Today we are on our way to Wichita, Kansas, where we will spend time teaching a room full of five hundred or so couples how to fight a good fight. And if there is one thing I know for sure, conflict is the price we pay in marriage for a deeper sense of intimacy as a couple. I know this because I have paid that price and won that prize. The connection I have with Les today, after three decades of married life, rests on the bedrock of authenticity and tenacity that can only be tested in the fires of conflict (good and bad, smart and dumb). And it's *that* kind of knowing that gives us credibility as teachers, not (as I once believed) the kind of credentials that come with never having fought.

And so when I mount the steps of a platform to teach these days, I am freer than ever to share moments of marital brilliance that only come following moments of marital bewilderment. Such as the one that happened recently, when after an exhausting weekend of speaking bookended by travel days with little sleep (or in Les's case, none at all), we were regrouping at home. Wanting to nurture Les back into a place of strength and rest, I served him his favorite healthy breakfast of oatmeal with a lavish assortment of nuts and berries. As he began to enjoy his meal, I announced I was tackling his laundry next, knowing this would add to his sense of well-being, getting his whole world back in order.

In response, Les simply looked up at me and began to clap — an exaggerated, slow-motion clap.

As I left the room, that impromptu applause filled my soul with utter bewilderment. I felt my tired cheeks grow hot, and the tears rimming my eyes began to fall. I wondered why on earth he would give me such a response, which looked for all the world like a *Saturday Night Live* sketch we had often laughed about together featuring the "sarcastic clapper." As I filled the washing machine, I told myself he didn't deserve my help. He could do his own laundry. Didn't he know how tired *I* was, how there were a million other little things I wanted to be doing with my time? How I work every bit as much as he does, and there was no reason either of us should assume this is my job? How I was trying with all my heart to choose love over laziness? Manual labor is a good outlet for anger, and I was stuffing and fluffing those clothes with great "enthusiasm."

Later, when I was feeling less fragile, I circled back to Les to confront him. My confused husband said, "What? My mouth was full of oatmeal when you told me you were doing my laundry, and I just wanted you to know how happy it made me, so I clapped."

Perception is everything. And even though I pride myself on being a highly intuitive person who reads her husband pretty well, and I might add, has finally mastered the mystery of discerning his dry wit (my mantra with Les for the uninitiated is "assume he's joking"), I had totally missed his motives. I cried again, this time from laughing. The relationship was once again repaired, and with every single repair our trust is deepened. Thus, the sarcastic clap caper had become the conflict that was my price tag for a deeper level of intimacy. Yes, I had paid the price. And yes, it was well worth it.

We are all pilgrims on this Jesus journey, and when it comes to the complexity of relationships, from feisty toddlers to bewildering marital meltdowns, what we most need are traveling companions who honor the complexity of our lives. Who get that exhaustion is real and perception is subjective and love is tears (both for laughter and for feelings of despair) and that sharing our unraveling can be the very thing that puts someone else back together again.

soul souvenirs

1. When has someone's honesty about the imperfection of her own life been a gift of encouragement to you? How have the imperfections of your life allowed you to connect with and encourage others?

2. In what ways has the fear of not being perfect or polished in your performance held you back from offering your gifts to others?

chapter 29

angels unaware

> *"For I was hungry and you gave me something to*
> *eat, I was thirsty and you gave me something to*
> *drink, I was a stranger and you invited me in."*
> MATTHEW 25:35 NIV

My friend Arlys grew up on a Christian missionary compound
in the heart of Muslim Tsanyawa, Nigeria. One of the vivid
memories of her childhood is her mother brewing and bottling
ice-cold root beer to offer to any warm and weary, dust-caked
traveler who stopped by. And the weary travelers did come.
Not just a handful either, but a steady flow of them. Between
fifty and a hundred guests a day would be graced by her sweet
carbonated refreshment offered in Jesus' name. Root beer was
a fun novelty, requiring only sugar cane and root beer extract
and yeast to create the carbonation. But it did require outra-
geous creativity (think *not* in the missionary training manual),
spirited hospitality, and the hard work of preparing and steril-
izing and bottling amidst the busy work of medical clinics and
teaching and the press of life. But it was root beer that became
the way into the hearts and minds of these dear people.

So I guess it's no surprise that Arlys herself is the very embodiment of hospitality and social grace. For three decades she used her considerable gifts in the public school classroom, where she taught home economics. Nowadays those gifts are relished by her friends and family, but certainly not confined to that inner circle. There is not a more interesting gathering than one you'll find at the Osborne home, where by her irreverent design elite insiders mingle with self-declared outsiders in a perfect blend.

So I think you'll understand how excited I was when my Aunt Jill gifted me with cooking lessons from Arlys for my fiftieth birthday. There is something holy about a shared meal. I think about how along the road to Emmaus the travelers walked and talked with Jesus for hours, sharing a deep discussion, but only after they sat down around a table, and Jesus blessed and broke and passed the bread, did they *know* him. Their hearts had been burning all along, strangely warmed as they talked, but sharing the table, the hospitality of wine and the bread, brought that awareness home to them, and they recognized him for who he really was.

That's what I want my life to be about—gathering people around tables that give them a huge dose of heart burn—not from my bad cooking, but the Road to Emmaus kind. Where strangers are invited into deep conversation and Jesus is present and bread is broken. Where grace is given, communion is formed, and deep conversation leads people to its Source.

So here I am at fifty taking cooking lessons for the same reason I once went to seminary—because I feel called. And because Arlys is not just an amazing cook but an incredible teacher, and because my Aunt Jill—who hates to cook so much she has a magnet on her refrigerator that says "I have a kitchen because it came with the house"—loves me enough to give me this gift.

Of course, the calling of hospitality has less to do with what's on the table and more to do with who's in the chairs. Any really good cook knows that. But if being relaxed and fully present at the table is my goal, I can't accomplish that without a certain level of confidence in my cooking.

And, what's more, hospitality is not about impressive culinary skills or a gourmet feast but about love and generosity shaped into nourishment. One of the most beautiful meals I've ever been served was a simple bowl of homemade rice and beans. The chef was a hard-working mom who cleaned buildings at Seattle Pacific University where I teach. When she learned that I had been put on bed rest with pregnancy complications, she began bringing me weekly servings of beans and rice, as she said, "For the baby." She had great confidence in the healing powers of her beans, a beloved staple she brought with her from her motherland, along with her thick South American accent and unhurried countenance. She took the only break she had all day, her lunch hour, to walk over to my home and deliver generous batches of unhurried conversation and well-seasoned beans. Her gifts warmed my heart at a time when life felt cold and disconnected from all certainty and sense of normalcy. She opened my eyes to God's presence in my stillness and turned my feelings of helplessness and isolation into purposeful solitude.

I'll never forget the first time I held that little baby, John, born three months before his due date. Weighing in at one pound and twelve ounces, and twelve inches in length, he was just a wisp of a micro preemie. His skin was nearly translucent. An IV delivered nourishment his digestive system wasn't ready to receive; a ventilator taped to his little mouth did the work of breathing his underdeveloped lungs weren't able to; and a monitor Velcroed to his tiny foot kept track of his tiny heart. For ten long days I could not even touch him.

Finally the day came. His neonatal intensive care nurse, Margaret, wrapped him up tightly in his swaddling blanket and gave him to me to hold for the very first time. My first thought in that moment might seem a bit irreverent. *I feel like I'm holding a burrito.* And maybe, in a way, I was. That miniature life sustained by nothing more than the prayers of loved ones and all those servings of beans.

In my smallish family of four I have every brand of appetite. My little burrito (who is now sixteen) is a picky eater (albeit much of this is scripted for him by his preemie-impacted physiology); my husband is mostly vegetarian (not by principle as much as preference); and my fifth grader is a bundle of culinary enthusiasm who typically has a dab of whatever he's just eaten (usually chocolate) smeared like a streak on the left corner of his smile. My friend Mia has said she will be disappointed if he doesn't have a streak of chocolate winging his smile on his wedding day.

All that to say, it can sometimes seem like an overwhelming project just to pull together a meal for my own family to enjoy together, much less one that stretches beyond the boundaries of our little quirks to embrace friends and strangers along our way. But I am feeling called to stretch. Not just beyond my culinary skills but my comfort zone, to create a lifestyle of hospitality that includes strangers as easily as friends.

I've always loved how Abraham's gracious hospitality to a stranger turned into an encounter with an angel. One never knows. And even though rainy Seattle is far from the dusty deserts of Africa or the Holy Land, I might just discover I've offered a cool drink to an angel, or that the "stranger" who is my guest is no less than my heart's Host.

soul souvenirs

1. How have you experienced a gift of hospitality that moved you deeply, helping you experience the communion of the saints? What happened, and what can you take away from that occasion into your current relationships?

2. How can you create space in your life for the grace of hospitality? Who can you welcome that wouldn't be expecting it but would be blessed?

chapter 30

lost and found

> *"We're going to feast! We're going to have a wonder-*
> *ful time! My son is here — given up for dead and*
> *now alive! Given up for lost and now found!"*
>
> LUKE 15:23 – 24

Yesterday my friend Mia found her long-lost wedding band
hiding deep inside a Converse tennis shoe. She was overjoyed,
and so were her family and friends. It had been missing for
days, and we had all participated in the search-and-rescue
efforts through our prayers if not in person. Because I love
Converse tennis shoes, and wear them nearly every day, Mia
credited my prayers as playing a lead role in the ring's discovery, which made me proud (even though we all know better).

Mia isn't the kind of person who holds tight to possessions.
She gives freely and shares everything she has. She is one of the
most resilient people I've ever known, taking her recent hys-
terectomy as well as her brush with thyroid cancer (and yes ...
surgery and radiation) all in stride. But the day she called about
her missing wedding band I could tell she was truly grieving its
disappearance for all the covenantal meaning it held.

Just a few days earlier, her iPhone had inadvertently fallen
from her oversized purse as she and the kids were rushing into
an evening church service. She didn't hear it fall nor did she see
it in the darkness on the asphalt curb. The next day it was just
gone. She had looked and looked for it with no results. But the
car that parked in that self-same spot after her *did* find it, with
its tires, as it crunched beneath the car's weight. So the lost
phone came back to her rendered useless. She didn't so much
mourn the loss of the phone as her ability to stay connected
to all of us, and the time she lost in the looking and replacing.

Then, mysteriously, her wedding band, which she only
ever takes off at night while she sleeps, seemed to vanish into
thin air. It felt like a vortex of loss. But of course, we already
know how the story ends. A Converse shoe turned ring bearer,
playing the starring role in this little ceremony of joy, uniting
Mia and her ring once again.

Loss can be a hassle (keys and phones); it can be sentimental (wedding bands disappearing or photographs destroyed); it
can be significant (a reversal of fortune: natural or manmade
disasters), or it can be monumental (failed marriages, devastating diagnoses). It's easy for me to write about Mia's loss
because although it was sentimental, even if the ring had never
been found, the covenant it symbolized is what truly matters,
and that wasn't lost. I have plenty of friends whose covenantal
relationships have been. Divorce and death are robbers of the
soul. Those losses, those black holes in our macro-universe,
are the ones that can send us spiraling into a vortex of doubt
and disconnection. Especially from God. It's been three years
since I lost my dear friend Kathy to cancer just days before her

fiftieth birthday; it's been nearly twenty since my own family dissolved with the divorce of my parents after thirty-five years of marriage (a loss that surprisingly hasn't diminished in its grief).

Jesus knew we could all relate to the experience of loss, so he told not one, or two, but three stories about lost things. A shepherd's life and livelihood was his sheep, and so without a second thought he went after a lamb lost in the wilderness (Luke 15:3–7). The poor woman had only a handful of coins, and so when one was lost, she followed it down every nook and cranny, lighting lamps and scouring dirt floors, until she found it (vv. 8–10). The father lost something even more beloved than the shepherd or the woman—a son who packed up and took off for a distant country (vv. 11–32). In this loss, the father knew there was nothing he could do but watch and wait. And he did exactly that. And "when [the son] was still a long way off, his father saw him. His heart pounding, he ran out, embraced him, and kissed him" (v. 20). There was a bath, a new outfit, and a feast. The banner at the party read, "Welcome Home!"

The surprise of these stories, of course, is when we realize that Jesus is teaching us about the vulnerability God chooses to feel toward us when we are lost to him. His aching desire for us to be found. His journey toward us in the wilderness, his willingness to follow us into every nook and cranny. His becoming light that we might be found within it. His ever-watching, forever-welcoming, heart-pounding love for us. He is the one who has known loss and longing—and that longing is for us. We are the ones who discover we can be found. And somehow this is what matters most. Even when we are in the black hole of hurt.

One day some friends who own a beach cottage on nearby Whidbey Island invited our son Jackson to take their dog on a long oceanfront walk. Afterward, Jackson said it had been the best day of his life. That dog had walked him home to his real self. From that moment on, Jackson began praying for a dog. Not a day passed by that he didn't pray. Before long he became an expert on breeds. He hung out at dog parks. Every nook and cranny of the universe seemed like a possible place for his dog to appear.

It was adorable, really. But heart wrenching for us. Living downtown on the seventeenth floor, we knew that caring for a dog would be no small thing. And we just couldn't find a way to move forward. But God responds to the simple, trusting faith of a child in the truest of ways. He sent a character into our lives named Bow Wow Bill, sort of a dog whisperer in the Seattle area. We told him exactly what breed we wanted, a dog that could love this unique city lifestyle: the ruby-coated Cavalier King Charles Spaniel. To his great surprise and ours, he just "happened" to have a Cavalier that needed a family, following the death of its beloved owner. In all of his years working with dogs, this was the only time he had ever had a Cavalier. Even Bow Wow Bill was amazed, sensing God at work.

And so Jackson got his dog: Charlie. Charlie, who was alone and needed a home in the worst way, though I doubt very much that he fully realized his plight. Nevertheless, Jackson's aching heart was filled that day with the coming of the dog he had been seeking through years of prayer and yearning.

It was a fullness of joy that has remained undiminished over time, so bonded are this boy and his dog.

Charlie is a gift to us all. In part because every time we look at him we see a dream come true against all odds, but mostly because of the way he comes to us all, expecting to belong and to be loved. He leans in, nudging his wet nose against us and turning his head to position his ears just right for a good rubbing. He cries with anguished joy at every reunion, his tail wagging his entire body. We know that Charlie considers us home. There have been losses in that little life, but that sweet creaturely heart is still wide open to us, welcoming of our love.

I don't want to take the analogy too far, but I think Charlie has taught me a lot about what it means to survive the crisis of loss. The key centers mostly on understanding that <u>God is my home, and that he longs for me with a love that goes beyond my capacity to grasp</u>. And no matter how monumental the loss (my dearest friend, my parents' marriage), it cannot reverse that heart-pounding love of homecoming and true communion. I simply have to lean in and position myself to receive it—heart wide open and trusting—and I will be found.

soul souvenirs

1. What glimpses have you caught of God's search to find you? How are you currently experiencing God's watching and waiting and celebrating your return?

2. How are you making yourself at home in God's love even in the midst of loss?

chapter 31

seawater and sun

Something of God which the Seraphim can never quite understand flows into us from the blue of the sky, the taste of honey, the delicious embrace of water whether cold or hot, and even from sleep itself.

C. S. LEWIS

A few years ago I developed a skin condition on my lower legs that was eventually diagnosed as psoriasis. Though the condition reveals itself on the surface of the skin, it is not a surface issue. The origins are embedded deep within my body, where my immune system, triggered by a threat, doesn't respond appropriately but instead overreacts, damaging the surface of my skin. It is a chronic condition and not curable. I have tried a host of topical treatments and therapies, yet nothing has helped. A girl who always relished the femininity of dresses, I have surrendered to a life of legs perpetually covered by pants. Occasionally the sadness of this loss creeps into my soul. This spring as I was dressing for a wedding, I broke down into sobs of shame over wearing slacks to such a special occasion. It's one of those things you can never explain to others, and so it sometimes makes me feel as if my very presence is disrespectful, showing up for the sacred moments of life in such cavalier costume.

After dealing with my disease for several years, it has recently, inexplicably, taken a turn for the worse, moving from just embarrassingly unsightly to constantly painful, irritating, itching, and burning—creating the need for an undercurrent of self-control to resist scratching, a self-control that is beyond my present reach.

The intensity of the struggle pushed me back into research mode for insight and suggestions on any kind of healing path. And it was in this process that I stumbled onto the unmistakable theme: the most successful intervention for healing psoriasis is seawater and sun. That's when it occurred to me that my Creator had woven into my DNA a disease whose very cure was spending significant time in the one place I loved more than any other on earth: the beach. The very thing I most desire to experience, the place in creation that I most longed for and felt compelled to enjoy and yet had created very little time for, was also the thing that offered healing not just to my spirit but to my body.

And so when my friend Clare invited me to join a group of dear friends at the beach in celebration of her fortieth birthday, I said yes without hesitation. Nestled together in a beach house aptly named "It's a Wonderful Life," we celebrated against the rugged beauty of the Washington Coast rimmed by great patches of old growth forest. For Clare, this was the culmination of wishing, dreaming, praying, and planning. She felt God had handpicked the invitation list, which she had prayerfully submitted to his direction. So rare is the time Clare has away from her consuming caregiving role as the parent of a special needs child, that every second is counted as treasure not to be squandered! I was honored to be on the guest list, and felt that my Great Physician had written me the perfect prescription for healing, too, even as I understood that each and every woman included had been handpicked by God's healing love in response to her own private need.

It was well into the night that we all bedded down. I found my place in a carriage house over the garage along with two other special friends, sleeping in a cozy nest of blankets on the sofa. The next morning the door creaked open in the predawn darkness, and a mirth-filled voice sang out, "Wake up, Leslie! We can sleep in heaven."

I shot up and out of my covers, pulled a coat over my jammies, very willingly took the warm cup of fresh coffee Clare handed me, and followed her along the forest pathway down onto the beach. The full moon shone so brightly as we walked that we had no fear of the dark, and when we emerged onto the beach, the sun began to rise behind us, with otherworldly colors filling the sky. Gone was the thick marine layer of clouds that had hovered there yesterday. The sky was as clear as glass. And together we stood there, between the moon and the rising sun — finding that God's love had filled our entire world from the east to the west.

And as we walked that morning, I thought about how even though our lives are broken by disease and disability, even still, we find ourselves immeasurably blessed.

There have been many hard moments for each of us since that day when God invited us to sit in box seats while the curtains between heaven and earth rolled back and the glowing orbs he created gave the performance of a lifetime. The psalm-ist saw this same show (it's been the longest-running hit in the history of the world), and cried out, "The heavens declare the glory of God; the skies proclaim the work of his hands. Day after day they pour forth speech; night after night they reveal knowledge ... Their voice goes out into all the earth, their words to the ends of the world" (Psalm 19:1–2, 4 NIV). Seawater and sun may heal psoriasis, but sun and moon can heal the soul, when what they reveal is the grandeur of the God who spun them into space, and ordained for the two of us this very time and this very place.

Clare calls me sometimes when she is feeling low and says, "Remember the beach that morning?" And she needs my memory to double hers. That's what we do when we gather, two or three of us, in his name. And what it stirs up within us and between us is akin to the kind of strength a Texan must have found in the embattled war cry, "Remember the Alamo."

Traveling saint Amy Carmichael, missionary from Ireland to India, who devoted her life to sheltering children caught in sexual slavery, expressed it this way after God's encouragement came to her simply through the sight of a particular tree:

> I have told of it — so very small a thing to tell at all when one considers what great things are happening in the world — because it may be that there are other roads in other lands and streets in many a town set with reminders of time which, if only we would let them remind us, would say, there, by that turning, as you went into that shop, as you saw that building or that tree by the wayside, in the multitude of the sorrows that you had in

your heart, the comforts of your God refreshed your soul. Fear not therefore, for He who was with you then is with you now ... For He often uses common things.[6]

And God used the seawater and the sunrise to strengthen our souls that morning, to plant the music of heaven within us. The apostle Paul puts it this way, "Do you see what this means — all these pioneers who blazed the way, all these veterans cheering us on? It means we'd better get on with it. Strip down, start running — and never quit! ... Keep your eyes on *Jesus*, who both began and finished this race we're in ... When you find yourselves flagging in your faith, go over that story again, item by item ... *That* will shoot adrenaline into your souls!" (Hebrews 12:1–3). Remembering God's presence in our past refreshes our sense of expectancy and fills our present with God's power.

soul souvenirs

1. Have you had an experience in your past, ordinary or extraordinary, that God used to refresh your soul? If so, what was it, and how can you draw strength from it?

2. When have you shared a time of spiritual communion with someone, and how did that change you?

6. *Learning of God: Readings from Amy Carmichael* (Fort Washington, Pa.: Christian Literature Crusade, 1986), np.

chapter 32

blaze

Go and set the world aflame.

ST. IGNATIUS OF LOYOLA

"Are you okay?"

"Sure, I'm just a little tired."

"No, I mean it; are you okay?"

Silence. Waiting.

"Why do you ask?"

"Well, I was praying for you right now; I mean, it's your day. And when I went to light your candle, well, it wouldn't light. I tried and tried, but no flame would come. So I got another candle and tried to light that one for you, and it lit up, but the flame was so dim it was barely there. That's when I knew it wasn't about the candle. I felt deep in my heart something was wrong. How are you, really?"

This is the call my friend received from her aunt, who had nurtured the tradition of lighting a candle for each person as she focused her prayers on them. Today was her niece's day, and her candle just wouldn't light.

The thing is, at the time, my friend was alone in her car,

driving and praying and sobbing. And she had cried out to Jesus, "Please, I need you. Show yourself to me."

And then from miles away, across the barriers of geography and probability, her candle wouldn't light. And then the call came. And it was a grace-filled conversation directed by the Holy Spirit. As she would explain one concern, her aunt would say, "Okay, but that's not all there is." And she would share more, and her aunt would say again, "I hear you, but that's not all." And finally, after the kind of deep listening that flows from the extravagant gift of time and undivided attention, she uttered a whisper of a thought from such a deep place it felt like she had turned her heart inside out. "That's it. God wants to heal that. Let's pray." And she felt the flickering flame begin to blaze.

St. John of the Cross calls those days when the candle won't light a "dark night of the soul." A poet, scholar, and mystic, he wrote a poem by that title, and many others while he was in prison for his faith. Although his life was dedicated to God, through teaching and serving the poorest of the poor, the letters he wrote from his dark prison days are his greatest legacy. John of the Cross was a Jesuit. The Society of Jesuits, an order of priests who define themselves as living in the company of Jesus, were founded by St. Ignatius of Loyola.

St. Ignatius came to his faith through his own fizzled flame. A Spanish knight preoccupied with conquest on the battlefield and with women, his life ground to a halt when his leg was shattered by a cannon ball, disabling him. Bored to tears during the long months of inactive recovery (which was never complete), he begged for some romance novels to read, but all that was available was a book about the life of Christ, which he grudgingly endured. As he read, his life slowly began to change in the direction of God until he found himself utterly transformed. His maiming had become his aiming: to walk, though limping, labored, and on unevenly measured legs, with God. At one point on his pilgrimage of faith he spent ten months in a cave, and the prayers he engaged in became the blueprints for the Spiritual Exercises that guide the Jesuits to this day. Finally, during an all-night prayer vigil, he knelt at an altar where he left his sword and knife, symbols of his own strength and pride, and humbled himself joyfully to a life of service to God.

Eventually his faith and leadership drew others who wanted to learn from him and live like him on their journey with Christ. This gathering of priests called themselves Jesuits. What distinguished Jesuit priests from others in their time was a calling to engage the world rather than to withdraw from it in monkish contemplation. As a group they took on a call to serve the whole person—spiritually, physically, emotionally, and intellectually. To this end, St. Ignatius commissioned them each with the call to "go and set the world aflame," warming this cold planet with passion for God.

They did go, and much of their work found expression in education. Eventually an explorer-priest found his way to the Pacific Northwest in the late 1800s and founded the Jesuit school, Seattle University. And in my late twenties, I found my way into this Jesuit school in pursuit of my doctorate, which played a significant role in the maturation and formation of my own faith. It was at Seattle University that I encountered Father Ronald Rolheiser, a professor who ignited a spark in my soul. I sat with a room full of graduate students in a third-floor, un-air-conditioned classroom. Windows were flung open toward the tree-lined inner courtyard on one side and the inner city on the other. The sounds of birdsong and traffic mingled with the professor's words: "As Christians we believe that we bear the image and likeness of God inside of us, and that this is our deepest reality. We are made in God's image. However, we tend to picture that somewhere inside us is a beautiful icon of God stamped into our souls. That may be well, but God, as Scripture assures us, is more than an icon. God is *fire-wild*, infinite, ineffable, non-containable."

Sitting there that day I felt like Timothy must have felt when he read his letter from Paul, who addressed him as "my dear son" with these warm words, "That precious memory triggers another: your honest faith—and what a rich faith it is, handed down from your grandmother Lois to your mother Eunice, and now to you! And the special gift of ministry you received when I laid hands on you and prayed—keep that ablaze! God doesn't want us to be shy with his gifts, but bold and loving and sensible" (2 Timothy 1:5–7). Yes, our fire-wild, infinite, ineffable, non-containable God doesn't sound like a timid or shy presence.

And I love it that Paul retells the story of how Timothy came to faith. How the flame that blazed in Timothy came from the faith of his *grandmother* Lois and his *mother* Eunice: two generations of women filled with the fire-wild presence of God, traveling saints helping Timothy along the Jesus journey. And I love it even more because my two great aunts were named Lois and Eunice, purposefully, after these women of faith, and along with my own grandmother Ophelia and my mother Kay, handed their faith down to me. All of us as women have the immense ability to fan the flames of flickering souls around us.

soul souvenirs

1. So often the brightness of our life comes as a result of our darkest days. How are you experiencing a power in your life that comes as a result of suffering?

2. When has the kindness and care of someone reached out to you in the midst of a dark time? How did they reach you, and what effect did it have? What would you like to emulate from that experience for your soul friends?

chapter 33

empty pockets

> *Dark is the world for me for all its cities and stars. If not for the certainty that God listens to our cry, who could stand so much misery, so much callousness?*
> ABRAHAM JOSHUA HESCHEL

No matter how much we are loved by family and friends, moments come to each of us when those who most love us and whom we most love in return, reach the limits of their capacity and leave us feeling alone, invisible, and completely misunderstood. This can be surprisingly painful, especially when our feelings are not for the others' lack of caring or concern.

First Samuel tells the story of childless Hannah, whose well-meaning and bewildered husband said to her, "Oh, Hannah, why are you crying? Why aren't you eating? And why are you so upset? Am I not of more worth to you than ten sons?" (1 Samuel 1:8). We've all been there, in that moment, when loved ones minimize our distress because it threatens to overwhelm them with its largeness, and they can't bear the load. They just want us to be okay but feel like we're saying they are not good enough to make us happy. But we *are* hurting and cannot make that hurt go away. So—not wanting to be another's source of pain—we must not only carry our distress but also bury it.

Hannah did this. As 1 Samuel 1 tells us, after weeping bitterly, Hannah pulled herself together and ate the family meal as a part of their shared worship experience. She did it and we do it too: pull ourselves together and share warm conversation even when we are troubled beyond words.

But when she could, Hannah slipped away to the temple, and once safely alone, she placed her crushed soul into God's hands. She poured her heart out in prayer. And so have you. You have laid out in prayer the unfulfilled desire of your deepest heart—the baby not conceived; the marriage not yet entered into or ended in crushing loss; the job you wanted but didn't get to pursue because your time and attention was needed at home; the job you cannot leave because your family's well-being depends on it; the diagnosis that you cannot accept. Maybe you stretched out prone on the floor in the privacy of your home, or took refuge in the safety of your shower as the waters poured down, disguising the sounds of your aching sobs. Or maybe you have entered into an empty sanctuary and knelt at the altar in solitude to pray.

Some prayers are visceral, coming from someplace beyond our mind. From the deepest chambers of our heart, they pass through our inmost being, rising like a lump in our throat. Sometimes we feel it so much that all sound is swallowed up within us and we can only move our lips, as Hannah did, when she knelt on the altar and poured her heart out to God. Her desperation for a child was so palpable, her silent prayers so filled with emotion that Eli the priest mistakenly thought she was drunk.

Some days we too are drunken with sorrow, our deepest longings welling up within us. Psalm 42 is a prayer for these very moments:

> *A white-tailed deer drinks from the creek;*
> *I want to drink God,*
> > *deep draughts of God.*
> *I'm thirsty for God-alive.*
> *I wonder, "Will I ever make it—*
> > *arrive and drink in God's presence?"*
> *I'm on a diet of tears—*
> > *tears for breakfast, tears for supper.*
> *All day long*
> > *people knock at my door,*
> *Pestering,*
> > *"Where is this God of yours?"*
> *These are the things I go over and over,*
> > *emptying out the pockets of my life.*
> > > (vv. 1–4)

There are days when we reach down deep and pull the pockets of our heart inside out and empty them. It's funny what we carry in our pockets. I was watching a scene from an old *Leave It to Beaver* episode with my son Jackson recently. June Cleaver is pulling things from Beaver's pockets before laundering his jeans. Ward Cleaver walks in and she points out the variety of curious items, including a dog tooth. When she asks Ward why in the world a boy would want to keep a dog tooth in his pocket, he thinks for a moment and then responds, "I don't know, but I do know that I wouldn't trust any boy who didn't want to."

I think God totally understands, and even delights in, the things we hold in the pockets of our hearts. And in doing so, he has great compassion for us when we turn them out. Memories and dreams, longings and desires. We carry these things around with us, saving them for the perfect time to pull them out and enjoy them. But often life doesn't work out that way. Our treasures cannot be saved up. Moth and rust do destroy. Thieves break in and steal. Divorce is one thief; disease is another. Even the natural process of aging steals the treasures of our youth (as this menopausal mama can personally attest). War, natural disasters, political strife, and corruption: all take their toll.

No one thinks for a moment that Hannah's barren womb is her own fault. She is both lovely and loved. Yet the pockets of her heart are turned out, emptied. And she lives on a diet of tears. And so she prays, thirsting for God-alive. She places her dream on the altar, asking God for his answer. And without knowing how God will respond, she gets up from the altar with a lightened spirit, a restored appetite, and a radiant glow to her face. She has emptied her pockets into the hands of God-alive, and he is holding her treasures now.

My friend Laura prayed the empty-pocket prayer for reasons similar to Hannah's. She and her husband, Richard, deeply longed for a baby to join their family, but after numerous devastating miscarriages and the encroaching reality of time and biology, the dream was dying. Like Hannah, Laura placed her dream on the altar before God. The answer to her prayers came in the form of sweet baby Rives, a darling little boy from China. My last text from her simply reads, "He is wonderful!!!! Absolutely the best decision ever for our family! Lovelovelove."

When Hannah's baby boy was born, she named him Samuel, meaning "God listened." Samuel became one of Israel's greatest judges, a priest and leader mentioned in the Hebrews 11 Hall of Faith. And it all started with Hannah's empty-pocket prayer, when the only One she could depend on to know her hurt and hear her heart was God-alive.

God does that. He works our wounds into a plan of redemption that reaches so far beyond us it becomes a part of the story he is writing in this world, a story that goes out from us to others in restoration and grace.

soul souvenirs

1. What are you carrying in the pockets of your heart that is so deep no one in the whole world seems to be able to understand it accurately?

2. How are you emptying the pockets of your heart in prayer? What gives you certainty that God is listening and that you have been deeply known and understood?

chapter 34

soul windows

There is a holy mystery in groups as words are spoken that open windows to the soul in another and all sit in awe and wonder. LARRY J. PEACOCK

Ten years ago I started a small group. It's a band of seven amazing and diverse women—wives, mothers, professionals. Women of faith who responded to the nudge of the Spirit and against rational analysis of their already overflowing calendars, entered together as a sisterhood of saints, offering friendship, prayer, and support that have sustained us all through a decade of life.

Together we have weathered the births of children and grandchildren; the achingly slow and the stunningly sudden deaths of parents and dear friends; seasons of failure and success, illness and health, astounding faith and searing doubt. We have paid tribute to life's milestones together: weddings, funerals, graduations, and retirements (Arlys retired after thirty years of teaching secondary education in the public schools and Joy after twenty-three years of homeschooling). There is more than a twenty-year age span between the oldest and youngest members of the group, and every one of us is deeply involved in different churches, with differing denominational loyalties and theological perspectives (one attends a church that sincerely believes the Bible teaches women are not called into church leadership; another is an ordained pastor). Even the grown daughters of our group marvel at the improbability of our bond and yearn to recreate it for themselves someday. Arlys, Bonnie, Joy, Lori, Sandy, Tami, and, of course, me. I introduced these fascinating women in my book *You Matter More Than You Think*, so I won't go into detail here, although I could write an entire book about each one of them.

Our conversations are rich and layered, built on both the direct intimacy of candid sharing and the indirect kind of knowing that happens over time in an environment of grace. We share what we are learning; we invite each other into our questions; we pray. Some days we bring a troubling dream to the table, in trust opening even our unknown selves to the group; other days we make ourselves the brunt of a shared joke, disclosing our foibles. And the laughter! It flows till we are gasping for air and mopping the tears: cheeks aching, tummies tormented, souls miraculously restored.

When Bonnie had a milestone birthday, Joy (living for a season in Washington, DC) arranged to be in Seattle to share our celebration. Being reunited for this festive occasion caused our spirits to burn bright. Bonnie had expressed a desire for nothing too serious (milestones can be so ominous), so we playfully donned coconut shells over our regular layers of T-shirts and jeans; added plastic leis, oversized straw hats, and imitation grass skirts; and threw her a joyously tacky celebration, oblivious to the innocent bystanders sipping their lattes, mochas, and macchiatos with dignity all around us. There was singing, candles, presents, and most of all — laughter. Thereafter, we assumed the nickname "The Coconut Club."

The laughter is good; even better are the moments of sheer brilliance, when someone is drawn to share. As a friend winds her way through the maze of thoughts and experiences before her, a collective warmth of recognition creeps around the room, causing us to exclaim, "Me too. That's exactly where I've been." God, in his infinite kindness, unifies us in moments of insight and shared growth that cause tiny hairs on our limbs to rise in unison while our hearts bow within us, breaking the bread of thanksgiving, drinking the cup of praise. Sharing in a communion of gratitude and growth.

Lately our group has become unified around the shared experience of waiting for God to act rather than taking matters into our own hands, especially when it comes to our children or our marriages. There have been symbolic dreams, collective tears; journals turned open on the table are read aloud. We have chosen to read certain books that guide us together along the path of patient waiting, and we have encouraged one another in persistent prayer.

Our group becomes a patch of earth where the kingdom of God is among us. I love how Jeremiah sees forward to the fullness of God's reign: "Thanksgivings will pour out of the windows; laughter will spill through the doors" (Jeremiah 30:19). And he might have added, "The windows of our souls will be opened by the love of God."

soul souvenirs

1. Where have you experienced the richness of diversity (age, stage, denominational or theological, personality) as a gift of communion?

2. Recall a time when you experienced God's presence in a powerful way in the midst of a group or gathering of friends. How did it create oneness among you?

benediction

"I've loved you the way my Father has loved me. Make yourselves at home in my love. If you keep my commands, you'll remain intimately at home in my love." JOHN 15:9–10

I'm so glad the New Testament is largely a collection of letters. This makes it so *personal.* And never more so than the final greetings that close each one. For example, the closing words of 2 Corinthians contain Paul's deepest heart for the believers in Corinth: "The amazing grace of the Master, Jesus Christ, the extravagant love of God, the intimate friendship of the Holy Spirit, be with all of you" (13:14). Amen.

Sometimes I feel like a walking paradox. On the one hand, I have found my life's "true place" in the way and life of Christ. On the other hand, I seemingly lack the hear-some-ness (that ability to listen and lean into the will of God), insight (depth of spiritual clarity), and courage (a quality of spirit that allows me to face difficulty without shrinking back) that are necessary for me to travel this journey with a deep consciousness of God. In my inner heart I want to tune in to the voice Isaiah talks about when he tells us, "Your teacher will be right there, local and on the job, urging you on whenever you wander left or right: 'This is the right road. Walk down this road'" (Isaiah 30:21). And I want to follow that guidance with reverent obedience. *Mostly.*

Jesus said to Peter at a dark point in his own journey toward the cross, "There is a part of you that is eager, ready for anything in God. But there's another part that's as lazy as an old dog sleeping by the fire" (Matthew 26:41). Peter knew and loved Jesus; he believed in him wholeheartedly; and yet still he slept through Christ's agony in the garden, and that was the least of his trilogy of failures that night. The fact remains that Peter loved Jesus deeply, which he later underscored with his trio of responses to Jesus' question, "Peter, do you love me?" Without hesitation he responded, "Yes, Lord, you know that I love you" (John 21:15, 16, 17). Peter was capable of both loving Jesus and contradicting that love *simultaneously.* And that, I find, is the crux of my paradox. Is it yours?

Some of us, like Peter, are heading to a place so deep into the kingdom that at one time or another, we will stretch out our hands and be led where we do not want to go (John 21:18). And still, our call in Jesus is to follow him and to love him. But how do we grow into that? I am convinced that as women, we grow into that by traveling the road together. Starting with our Quest, responding to God's Calling, hanging onto him during our Crises, and eventually following God's love into the depths of Communion with our creator, redeemer, transformer, and friend—all in the company of the sisterhood of traveling saints, who share the profound privilege of walking each other Home.

Just yesterday I had coffee with a circle of friends who

have been showing up for each other weekly for six years. Our common thread in the beginning was that we each had a child starting kindergarten at the same school (now those children are fifth graders). Our plan was simple and stress free: meet for coffee directly following morning school drop-off every Wednesday at the corner Starbucks (where, by the way, the mayor of Shoreline, a Seattle suburb, also doubles as barista, which is probably the single most strategic campaign move any mayor in the Seattle area could ever make).

From the start, our understanding was simple: Come when you can, no need to notify if you can't. No guilt, all grace. Funny thing, we come. Rain or shine, we come. Well-put-together and completely-falling-apart, we come. We find an angle and celebrate everything ... new homes or jobs or days free of principal office visits, jeans that fit. Last days of diets of any kind, including cleanses. Drinking in the coffee or the tea and, even more, the communion. Our common thread now is less our children and more the bond we have created between us by just showing up for one another over time.

In the midst of our lively give-and-take on this morning, I had commented offhandedly to my friend Laurra that she responds to the inner nudges of the Holy Spirit more readily than any friend I know. Knowing Laurra has taught me much about knowing God. When Jesus saw Philip's friend Nathanael coming toward him, he said, "There's a real Israelite, not a false bone in his body" (John 1:47). Which is a perfect description of my girlfriend Laurra: a real Christian, not a false bone in her body. In fact, Laurra, who came to faith as an adult, attends a church with a more charismatic emphasis than mine. Recently a guest preacher with a gift of prophecy came to lead worship, speaking words of insight over many in the church. When he came to Laurra, his comment to her was, "Here is a person who is guileless." Honest, straightforward, and expecting exactly that in return from anyone she meets. Bull's-eye.

And with that authenticity, which includes the purest love for Jesus I've encountered in a sister of Christ, comes an unguarded vocabulary that might make a Seattle longshoreman feel right at home. So although she doesn't consider herself any kind of a saint (except on rare days when she doesn't use the f-word as frequently and she eats only whole foods), on this day at the corner Starbucks she received the compliment without fanfare, and off the conversation went in a new direction.

It wasn't until the afternoon pickup time, sitting in the carpool lane, that I was able to listen to my phone messages. The one from Laurra recounted an experience immediately following our time together that morning. She had been in a hurry to stop by "Fuzzy Buddies" to drop off her dog to romp with other canine friends while she was out for the day. It was raining hard (imagine that in Seattle), and she had been appalled to witness a driver in front of her pull into the flooded far right lane for no other reason than the thrill of sending a tidal wave of dirty rainwater splashing onto an elderly man helplessly waiting curbside at the bus stop. No sooner had she passed than the thought *Do something for him* came to her. She brushed it aside, until she recalled my comment about Holy Spirit nudges from our earlier conversation. *This is a nudge; I need to listen.*

So she did a U-turn, pulled slowly up to the curb, got out feeling hesitant and extremely silly, and said, "I saw what happened to you just now, and I felt terrible about it. I just thought you could use a warm drink after that cold splash." Then she handed him a Starbucks gift card.

"Wow," he said, "it's been forever since I had one of those. But what about her?" he said, pointing to an obviously well-appointed woman in business dress. "She's had it happen to her plenty too."

So Laurra handed him a booklet of Starbucks cards and said, "Well, why don't you take these and share them with whoever you feel needs them." They exchanged warm smiles, and off she went.

When she called, her comment to me was this: "It was your words this morning that gave me the courage to do it, to believe it was God speaking and obey."

I took a deep breath. *Thanks for saying that,* I thought. *I was the one who was so blessed by the whole thing.*

And here is the deep truth: I frequently drive that same road, and had on that very day cringed when witnessing a nearly identical scene, and yet responded to nary a nudge from the Holy Spirit in the wake of it. And so my words that went out to her came back to me bearing fruit of future obedience in my own life; each of us is helping to fill the other's journey with a deeper consciousness of God. And that is the whole of it: soul friends traveling the right road together, a sisterhood of traveling saints, walking each other Home.

You have been invited into deep-spirited, soul-altering friendship, into a communion with the sisterhood of traveling saints walking the Jesus journey all around you. Join or create a small group; open your heart to a new friend; pick up the biography of a saint whose life can become a hidden guide; show up in hospital corridors and at bus stop encounters with strangers. Talk to tattooed baristas; open your eyes to the miracles of God's grace in the people he has placed all around you. Every time you move someone from the periphery to the center of your heart, you are making the presence of God visible in this world, and you are making the love of God your *home*.

You Matter More Than You Think

What a Woman Needs to Know about the Difference She Makes

Dr. Leslie Parrott

Are you longing to make a difference?

A season of soul-searching walks along Discovery Beach in Seattle revealed a secret far too many women never find. In this heartfelt book, Leslie Parrott reveals a personal message sure to keep you from looking at the pieces of your life as mere fragments scattered to and fro by any impulsive tide. Rather, you will soon see that the random fragments of your life—whether it's doing laundry, dashing to the store, tending to either your kids or a full-time job (or both)—mean something.

The random pieces of your life hold great potential for making a profound difference.

With the help of her Band of Sisters, Leslie shows you how to take the improvised moments of your own life and create a worthy composition of more value than you imagined. You're already making a difference, and the more you understand this difference, the bigger that difference will be.

Whether you are married or single, restless or content, wounded or strong, this book, designed for every woman who longs to be more than part of the mainstream, is for you.

Available in stores and online!

Love Talk

Speak Each Other's Language Like You Never Have Before

Drs. Les and Leslie Parrott

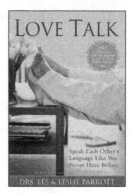

Love Talk is like no other communication book you've ever read. The fruit of years of research by two foremost relationship experts (who also happen to be husband and wife), this book forges a new path to the heart of loving conversation. You'll begin by identifying your security need and determining your personal communication style. Then you'll put together everything you discover to learn how the two of you can speak each other's language like never before.

This very day, you can begin an adventure in communication that will draw the two of you closer, and closer, and closer ... consistently, in a way that creates the depth and connection you long for in your relationship.

Love Talk includes:

- The Love Talk Indicator, a free, personalized online analysis for determining a person's unique talk style (a $30 value)
- The secret to emotional connection
- When not to talk
- A Communications 101 primer
- Practical help for the "silent partner"
- Designed for use with the companion men's and women's Love Talk workbooks (sold separately)

Available in stores and online!

THIS CHANGES EVERYTHING
SAVING YOUR MARRIAGE BEFORE IT STARTS
+
SYMBIS ASSESSMENT

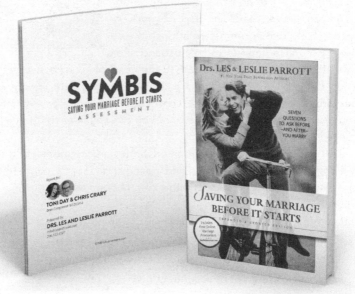

More than a million couples have used our award-winning *Saving Your Marriage Before It Starts* (SYMBIS for short) and now — through the new SYMBIS Assessment — we can help couples prepare for lifelong love like never before.

SYMBISAssessment.com